A LITTLE SCHOOL ON THE DOWNS

Harriet Finlay Johnson, 1910.

A Little School on the Downs

The story of pioneer educationalist Harriet Finlay Johnson headmistress of Sompting School, West Sussex 1897-1910

MARY BOWMAKER

Woodfield Publishing

First edition, published in 2002 by

WOODFIELD PUBLISHING
Woodfield House, Babsham Lane, Bognor Regis
West Sussex PO21 5EL, England.

ISBN 1-903953-30-8

This book is dedicated to
Jean Bather
my close friend and confidante
over many years
and to
Peter R Bowmaker
my beloved husband

Sompting pupils re-enact the coronation of William & Mary.

Pupils making a vegetable garden.

Contents

Girls using reading books from the school library (*see p.29*).

Boys working to make a shed in the school grounds (*see p.29*).

Acknowledgements

My thanks to:

Daphne Morrison, fellow student and friend who introduced me to the work of Harriet Finlay Johnson, thus providing me with countless happy hours of research and study, and the joy I have found in writing this book.

Dorothy Heathcote, our senior lecturer at the University of Newcastle-upon-Tyne, an inspiration and a friend, and the real promoter of the work of Harriet Finlay Johnson over many years. To Dorothy and Roger Barnes, thank-you for making the course so enjoyable and the work such fun.

A.T. Ternent whose earlier study of Harriet Finlay Johnson and her school was invaluable to me in the research.

E.G. Riby, headmaster of White Styles School, Sompting, for his generous help on my first visit to Sompting and for giving me complete and free access to the school log books.

Miss Elsie Weller, a former scholar at the school and Harriet's sister-in-law, was especially helpful and forthcoming in the information she gave me. Untiring during long interviews, and corresponding with further information, she readily gave permission for use of any relevant material – including private papers, and photographs – she had in her possession.

Sussex local and National Newspapers; to various libraries including: West Sussex County Council and Worthing Area Library; West Sussex Record Office, Chichester. The National Meteorological Library & Archive and Newcastle-upon-Tyne University.

Dr. John Fines, Historian, for his valuable time and assistance; to former scholars at Harriet's school whose vivid memories gave substance and reality to this work; the villagers at Sompting who made me welcome;

Rachel Brown my 'splendid' typist; and to my husband Peter for his unflagging help and encouragement.

A nature study game at Sompting School, c.1900. Agnes Peters (see p.127) is the tall girl standing at the back.

I. *The Time ~ 1887-1910*

Between the years 1897 and 1910, an educational experiment was carried out in Sompting School West Sussex that had worldwide repercussions. The experiment, hailed as the 'true gospel of education' by the then Chief Inspector of Schools, E.G. Holmes, involved almost the whole village as we see for the first time Community Education, the Integrated Day and Education through Drama.

Harriet Finlay Johnson, headmistress of Little Sompting School from 1897 to 1910 and author of the book *The Dramatic Method of Teaching*, was the pioneer who led the way in this progressive method (of teaching), and whose work was acclaimed in places as far away as America and Japan.

Discovering Harriet's book some years ago and aware of its significance educationally, socially and historically, I was determined to make an in-depth study of the work. The book, photographs, the school log-books, material from writers and reporters, and taped interviews with former scholars, some in their late eighties, made retracing those 'halcyon' days of 'Merry England' as they were described, a joy. It proved to me that there is nothing new. People remain basically the same, no matter in which century they have lived.

The advances of the time technologically were as startling and as revolutionary in their day as the oncs that we are experiencing now, the Victorians having produced more inventions than any previous century. The world was suddenly aware of many new wonders in science. It was jolted out of its long slumber into strange sights – cars, trains, aeroplanes, and new sounds: the wind-up gramophone, wireless telegraphy, moving pictures. Wonders were being experienced in many spheres of life and over many parts of the world.

Harriet Finlay Johnson was 'alive' enough and 'educated' enough to go along with these great events. She took an interest in all facets of life and therefore took the school, indeed the whole village, along with her. For a young women, especially in those times, to make a stand alone, and go against so many of the practices in schools that had been perpetuated for generations required tremendous courage. And for the people of Sompting, young and old alike, to have the vision and the 'will' to support her and make the great experiment possible, was admirable in itself.

With respect and barely contained excitement I tried to re-enter the Victorian age on my visits to Sompting. I stood in the doorway of the old schoolroom looking out at the elm tree as it guarded the path, a silent witness to the many lessons and plays acted out beneath its boughs. Observing a play group busily employed within, I recalled that Harriet Finlay Johnson must have stood on this same spot fondly watching children of a by-gone age, as they too actively engaged themselves in a school so far ahead of its time that one of the educators of the day, on reading about it was inspired to write 'it was like the discovery of a new world'.

I could have been in a time warp as I stared at present day children, but in my minds eye saw only those others. Girls with huge white pinafores over calf length black dresses, wearing black stockings in high, tightly laced black boots, with long flowing hair and eager expectant faces, would scuttle their way to the school in Loose Lane. Young lads wearing breeches and dark shirts under waistcoats or jackets, flat caps perched jauntily on heads that were, to some villagers anyway, getting ideas above their station, hurried along to the school as though to some new game, or adventure, or compelling excitement.

And what of this wonderful place that boy and girl alike were eager to reach? It was far from the usual Victorian school, with old dreary rooms housing row upon row of benches and desks; an ever-pervading atmosphere of drudgery and gloom and overall, the persistent threat of punishment, depending simply on the whim of an impatient teacher. The school in Loose Lane was a revelation. One reporter, from the Morning Leader wrote:

> *'Perhaps Sompting is the only village in England where the children cannot be kept out of school'.*

In all this 'bubbling atmosphere' and 'collective activity', Harriet Finlay Johnson never wavered in her main concern, which was the welfare and happiness of her scholars. We remember, particularly, the young lads who forged their ages shortly after leaving Sompting School to fight and die in the First World War. It is good to think that they had at least experienced a little share of happiness as many of their exploits and adventures, dancing before our eyes in the school log books, would have us believe.

But it is sad to reflect that at the height of her career, Harriet had to resign her position as Headmistress, on her marriage to George Weller, a resident of Sompting and seventeen years her junior.

She was, and through her, the people of Sompting were, celebrities, unwitting pioneers of an integrated life-style now known as the 'community'.

The fact that their light disappears, then suddenly re-appears, through the mist of time, as various generations of scholars and writers read and re-read and discuss those 'enchanting' days assures us that, strange as it may seem, a small school in a little Sussex village can impress the world, and bequeath, by example, a legacy of inestimable value.

II. The Place ~ Sompting, West Sussex

June 1897. The world was suddenly a smaller place. New technology, on the verge of erasing the old order, would change life and herald the dawning of a new age. Soon, the comforting sound of horse's hooves reverberating over cobbled stone streets would be gone. Familiar sights and sounds and smells drift away, and people, especially in the towns, harbour feelings of expectancy and hope for a better tomorrow.

Early in the same month three fashionable ladies made a journey. They travelled sixty-six miles by train at a cost of 5/6d per person first class, from their comfortable home in Hampstead, London, to start a new life in the tiny village of Sompting, West Sussex. Harriet Finlay Johnson, the newly appointed headmistress of Sompting school, her sister Emily, appointed as an assistant teacher at the school and their mother, Jane Ann Finlay Johnson, originally from Cavan, Ireland, who would live with them and 'keep house'. Their journey took them from Hampstead, across London to Victoria, then to Brighton on the London and Brighton South Coast Railway. From Brighton by train to Lancing where the Vicar, the Reverend Robert E. Williams, met them with a pony and trap that carried them along three miles of rough country roads to the schoolhouse in Loose Lane.

How anxious they must have felt as each mile took them further from the city they loved to an uncertain future in a quiet village. Leaving a London bubbling over with excitement as it prepared for Queen Victoria's Diamond Jubilee Celebrations to be held on June 22nd, a London full of foreigners, of flags and bunting, soldiers shiny in their ceremonial dress, rich rubbing shoulders with poor. As one commentator put it, 'preparations for the Jubilee filled the public mind to the exclusion of everything else'.

The weather during that June month of 1897 was similar over the southern half of England; more rainfall than usual, but the sun shone for longer periods and more brightly giving an unusual warmth. There the similarity between the big city and tiny village ended. In London, doors and windows opened almost every day onto some new wonder of science, while in Sompting, things remained the same.

Sompting, West Sussex, at the turn of this century, was occasionally labelled barren and uninteresting. The villagers, of a quiet nature, plodded on, neither moaning about their lot nor getting excited over the few nice things that might happen to brighten otherwise dreary lives. Hard working and practical, they had little time for daydreaming or pondering on future possible changes. Their footsteps trod the same highways and byways that their forefathers trod for countless centuries past. A living was made from farming, nurseries, market-gardening and from greenhouse, or to use the older term, 'glasshouse produce'. Sompting has always been in the lead in glasshouse culture. There were glasshouses at Rectory Farm Sompting, early in the second half of the last century and it was also known in the 19th century for its orchards and particularly its fig trees, which were sheltered by high flint walls. Men worked on the land and women did seasonal work such as fruit picking. The girls were often absent from school to stay at home 'minding babies' and doing household chores. Boys did jobs such as holding the horse's head when the farmer was ploughing, and bird scaring with a clapperboard. It was a close-knit community. Strangers in the village soon learnt to be discreet when they realised that most of the inhabitants were related and did not take easily to new faces.

A centre of settlement named Sompting was recorded in the 11th century. The most popular meaning of the word 'Sompting' is 'dwellers at the marsh', but other explanations go back even further than the Doomesday Book. The name, of Saxon origin, has survived, with changes in spelling and pronunciation through all the changes of nearly fifteen hundred years of history.

Snuggling at the foot of the South Downs, Sompting stands on wide stretches of downland, uneven paths criss-cross weaving their way to brooks and sea. A network of brooks and drains separated Sompting from the seashore, spanned by wooden bridges for cattle to cross from one pasture to another. A stream known locally as the River Ditch, or by its older title of Broadwater Brook was once a considerable waterway. The southern end was possibly used as a harbour where, in the Middle Ages, it is believed boat building was carried on.

Lying west of Brighton, on West Street, the Old Chichester, Brighton Road, the village followed the typical pattern of parishes in Sussex at that time. Isolated farmhouses standing boldly alone, bragging by their solitary stance a fearlessness and independence that had remained undisturbed for centuries. Farming on the Downs merged onto the plain. A church standing halfway up the slope dominated the village.

Sompting Parish Church, St. Mary's, is famous for its Saxon architecture and for its links with the Crusading Order of fighting monks, the Knights Templar. The Order had almost disappeared by 1308 and in 1312 the Church forcibly dissolved it. In 1324 the Pope assigned all templar property to another Order of Crusades, the Knights of St. John. The Knights, often known as the Hospitallers, are best known today for the work of the Ambulance Brigade. A fair held on July 5th, the feast of the Nativity of St. John the Baptist (which survived until the beginning of the present century), reaffirmed the link with its history of mystical significance between the Order and the village. A record of a property transaction in the area informs us that, in 1318:

> *'Adam Ayleth settled on John de Patenay and his wife Lucy, Adam's daughter, a dwelling house with outbuildings and land at a rent of a rose on St. John's day'.*

It is surprising to find four manors listed in a village of Sompting's size in Norman times, but some of them were very small. The present manor of Sompting Abbotts, a handsome building set in a frame of trees, sits slightly higher on the hill than the ancient church. Rebuilt towards the end of the last century on the site of a succession of predecessors, the manor played an important part in May Day celebrations, which were a feature of village life.

In a log book entry for April 26th 1876, we read of the children practising songs for May Day. An entry dated April 30th 1901, when Harriet Finlay Johnson was headmistress tells us of a '*half day holiday to gather flowers for May Day*'. A 'living memory' of two elderly ladies is getting up early one bitterly cold May Day. It snowed during the morning and the children had to shelter in a building at Upton Farm. The Worthing Gazzette, in an article dated May 2nd 1906 presents a picture of the celebrations, which hardly varied over the years:

> *'Sompting seems to be the only place in the immediate neighbourhood in which the pretty custom of celebrating May Day is maintained. Yesterday about 135 of the school children assembled in the playground and from there marched to Sompting Abbotts'. Each child was supplied with a sash, rosette and flag and they marched through the village singing songs led by the May Queen and her maids of honour, who were accommodated in a decorated cart drawn by a decorated donkey.*

> *The children were regaled en-route with home-made buns and new milk. Three pretty items were the decorated soap-box carriages of the boys, one decked with cowslips and drawn by a rope of daisies, and another representing a machine gun with a khaki clad attendant'.*

From mysticism to smugglers, the history of Sompting, bearing in mind its reputation as a particularly small, quiet place is certainly varied. During the early part of the 19th century when smuggling was at its height and widespread along the Sussex coast, the men of Sompting took their fair share of the business. The Brewers Arms Inn was formerly an old house called 'The Smugglers', dating from the 16th century, and although there is no hard evidence that smugglers used it, there are rumours about tunnels in Sompting.

Those who did not participate in the actual exercise of smuggling were content to turn a blind eye to the proceedings. When the smugglers needed horses to haul in their cargoes, they took them from any nearby stable. If it was June, haymaking time, or August with corn to be reaped, and the farmer found his horses stabled but tired and sweat-stained from a night out with the 'gentlemen', he asked no questions. Any annoyance he may have felt was quickly dispelled by a keg of brandy for himself or bottle of French perfume for his wife which he would find in the manger. Smuggling it appears continued until well past the middle of the last century.

For all its agreeableness, Sompting has offered little attraction to the famous as a place of retreat or residence. The only Royalty to have visited was Queen Caroline, consort of George IV, who stayed at Sompting Abbotts in 1814 before embarking for the continent. Author and traveller E.J. Trelawny, a friend of the poets Byron and Shelly, moved to Sompting in 1870 and died there in 1881. And in the mid 17th century, George Sowton, a Sompting butcher, was in much demand as a magician and healer.

Village life centred around one narrow main street, West Street. Serving a population of under 700, its general store-cum post-office was a house next to Trelawny's cottage. The store was a hive of activity by day, the focus shifting after dark to the attractions of three public houses, The Marquis of Granby, The Gardeners Arms, and The Brewers Arms.

In 1897, nine private residents were listed and commercial residents who included:- Miss Annie Grover, beer retailer whose business was conducted from a house; George Goatcher, the shoe-maker; William Weller, the Wheelwright and Richard Ayres, Blacksmith. Charlotte Kennard was a milk-lady in the area. She pushed an iron milk trolley complete with churn and milk cans, 1 pint and ½ pint. Two cottages were built in 1876 for the benefit of the aged and infirm by the Penfold sisters, Jane and Clara, in memory of their brother John.

There were nine farms and a large number of market gardens. Rows of dwelling houses belonging to different farms had a bake-house in the row that sold bread, and a communal toilet that stood alongside the bake-house.

The land south of West Street, just above the blacksmith's shop, was one large meadow for cows. Slightly lower lay allotment ground and below this the brook-land that led down to the sea. It was possible to walk to the sea from the southern tip of the village, one third of a mile away.

Walking was a popular pastime. It was the cheapest and sometimes the only way to travel. The public footpaths and little rough tracks over the Downs being much used both for pleasure and for the privacy they afforded when courting. For most people, evenings were spent reading, playing cards or visiting friends. There was a ladies glee club, a band with brass instruments, bugles, bass drum and a string double bass; the band shed was next to the school wall. There were cricket and football matches on Saturday afternoons but no pitch at this time.

Newspapers were dropped off a train at Lancing Station then collected and delivered by children pulling soapboxes on wheels (bogies). Medicines were put on a train to Lancing, the village doctor collecting them as he travelled around by horse and trap.

Oil could be bought in the village but villagers shared produce (a pig would be cut up and shared out at Christmas time), and relied mainly on the visits of tradesmen for their supplies. Horse-drawn tradesmen's carts would arrive beautifully painted, some quite elaborate. The baker's cart called two or three times a week, and the market gardener's cart called after he had been to Brighton market.

A number of people made one trip a year to Brighton to buy clothes and other necessary items. They would take a horse and trap to Lancing, then travel by train to Brighton. Travel was by trap or bicycle but apparently you were lucky if you had a bicycle. At Worthing, a big grocer catered for well-off people. Orders were collected by a messenger on a bicycle and delivered by a man with a horse and cart.

Typical of these Downs-edge villages is that they liked their schools and village halls to be built at a distance from the people they were to serve. When in 1889 the owner of Sompting Abbotts manor built a village hall (called the Reading Room), he put it a quarter of a mile from the main centre of population.

Just below the church and a wooded plantation, on a site called Loose Lane, lived the school. Built in 1872, isolated, with fields opposite and only one row of cottages for company, it was a target for all weathers. Facing the sea, some three miles away, strong winds and gales not infrequently whistled and howled as they swept over desolate Downs charging towards the solitary building. Fierce rain storms beating against sturdy roof and walls, deep drifting snow blocking lanes and tracks that led to the school were often the subject of entries in log books over long years.

A series of repairs to the school and school-house carried out and entered in a log book for September 6th 1886 gives us a glimpse of the state of the building at that time.

September 6th 1886;

> *'During the holidays, the interior of the school has been renovated. The lobbies, out offices, etc. painted and white-washed. The brick floor of the kitchen in the schoolhouse has been taken up and a boarded floor substituted. The set of desks (three) used by the first class children has been made more secure and better for writing as by being mounted on whole wooden blocks'.*

A knapp-stone building with adjoining schoolhouse, the boys and girls playgrounds were located behind the school, probably to give shelter from inclement weather. Separate boys and girls cloakrooms and toilets had their own doors, which led into the schoolroom from the yards. The only other entrance was by a side door and porch, which also led directly into the schoolroom. This schoolroom, which was the main area in the building, measured 20ft x 30ft, and the classroom next to it, used by the infants, 20 x 20 ft. By 1897 these same rooms housed up to 130 pupils, some of whom walked four miles each way to school and home again.

The teachers enjoyed living accommodation in a spacious schoolhouse. A two-storey building, it had three bedrooms upstairs. Downstairs contained a large living room, which, according to the custom of the day, was used only on Sundays, or 'special' days. A large kitchen, the hub of the house, included a long kitchen range. Also downstairs was a toilet, pantry and scullery. By 1900 the scullery had a brick floor and a sink for washing clothes; water was heated on the kitchen range. Clothes were hung out to dry in the back yard where a small garden stretched beyond the yard and down the side of the house. The schoolhouse paraded a front door, seldom used, and a back door, which, after walking along the back of the school, led into the schoolroom via the children's entrance.

There was no doubt that Harriet Finlay Johnson would adapt and be 'at home' in Sompting. She had the character plus determination to meet any challenge successfully. The fact that here, on her doorstep, lay the ideal terrain to satisfy her deep love of nature, and the opportunity to pursue the joy she found in walking, was perhaps, fate. In this area of foothills, with flatlands stretching seawards and abounding in brooks and streams, she would find contentment; contentment in the peace, the stillness, the quiet. In the beauty and diversity of nature, which she would later acknowledge as the source of inspiration for her pioneering work in the school.

Harriet had left behind her the 'roller-coaster' society of the Victorian age; a society rushing headlong into the future. A society living in an era of rapid change and divide, with its extremely rich and pauper poor; a society with its pride of

Empire yet hate of materialism; a society living in an age of faith and an age of doubt, with no consistent attitude to anything.

The tranquillity of the countryside infiltrating the schoolhouse would encourage a depth of silence, a healing balm, never experienced before by city ladies. A silence so 'dynamic' in its ever-pervading presence, it could almost be 'touched'. A silence broken only by the inevitable ticking clocks, an important feature of every Victorian household.

Pupils hold up their drawings of holly berries for Christmas cards. This day became known for 'the big holly berry fight' that took place in the schoolroom on 20th December 1905. Thomas Bashford is seated far left. The boy sitting next to him has a black eye! (see p.31)

III. The Cast ~ but not in order of appearance

To look back on scenes long since gone, straining to peer ever more closely through the door marked 'past', can be a tantalising yet satisfying experience. We soon realise that there is nothing new; that people are basically the same no matter in which century they have lived, or perhaps will be born to live in, and that the 'play' of life, their interaction with others, is an amazing network, a series of connections which lead, divert, circle fate, in some major or minor way.

Striving to re-create the reality of a by-gone age can be a daunting task. To touch the heart of a person, to reach out to their very 'being', especially over a long time span, some would say is impossible. Yet there are individuals whose life, whose existence, cries out to be heard and to be understood. Such a one is Harriet Finlay Johnson.

Born at Hampstead on March 12th 1871, she lived with her mother and younger sister Emily. There were other sisters who had died of typhoid and Harriet herself suffered from the disease in her teens. Her father, a master builder, was killed tragically. Perhaps the need for money to support the family forced her to teach full-time while studying at night and on a Saturday morning to obtain a Teachers Certificate. It is believed that she had a romance while studying for her Teachers Certificate, the evidence being in a romantic short story she wrote at that time which was thought to be autobiographical. She passed her Certificate Examinations (second division) in 1892, and received the certificate itself two years later. Emily was trained for laundry and domestic work.

Both sisters have been described as 'nice looking'. Harriet had a shapely, slight figure, was of average height, with sandy coloured hair, always stylishly coifed. It was only discovered in her forties that she wore a wig, probably from the effects of the typhoid illness suffered in her teens. A tradesman saw her without the wig through her kitchen window in Sompting, and of course...

Having taught at St Mary's C of E school, Willesden, for eight years, and then for a short time under the Tottenham School Board, Harriet Finlay Johnson took up her appointment as Head Teacher at Sompting School on June 14th 1897. Emily was appointed to work in the infant department as an assistant teacher.

The village of Sompting must have seemed small and remote to the family after life in London. Artistically talented, Harriet was an excellent pianist who also excelled in drawing. We see her sense of occasion in the sensitive way she wrote numerous entries in the Sompting School log books. Among the villagers she was perceived as *'aloof'*, *'looked every inch the headmistress'*, *'she knew what she was about'*, *'she had a sharp tongue when needed*'. But in contrast to these perceptions is the loving way in which, in her late thirties, she drew a heart around a photograph of her future husband, George Weller.

Emily Finlay Johnson.

Emily was thought of as being more friendly, yet in the work at Sompting School, Emily was the one remembered for caning the infants, while Harriet was remembered as being loving, caring and unsparing of herself in her devotion to the children. Former scholars have stressed the fact that she wanted the children to be happy and that she was a 'natural teacher'.

'*We all do our best when we are happy*', was a thought she expressed many times, and '*childhood should be our happiest time, absorbing big stores of sunshine for possible future dark times*'.

She never forgot her own happy childhood and the history stories acted with her chums after school hours. She was concerned with the integration of educational experience and the dramatic method was one of her, if not the teaching aid. No one knows when or how she devised her dramatic method of education. Perhaps it evolved from memories of her own school days.

Harriet was aware of, and respected, the child as an individual. She was concerned for the child's growth, and saw this growth as an 'all-round' development, a preparation for life. She was aware of the importance of language development and of speech training; but the lessons of language development, and speech training must occur naturally, within the material of the play or the activity, or the lesson. She is the first teacher we know of who uses drama as a learning medium without reference to audiences.

Harriet Finlay Johnson had many problems to overcome – local opposition could be expected if anything new were attempted – and many masters to please. In her thirteen years as Head Teacher at Sompting School she set about creating an environment of happiness which would, in turn, breed well-being, and, cause and effect being what it is, within the framework of these 'right conditions', her pupils had the freedom to grow, and therefore to 'learn' in a completely new way.

She touched on possibly every desirable aspect of education in her book, 'The Dramatic Method of Teaching'. Its breadth and vision are inspiring. Early on in its pages she explains her thoughts, that it was her endeavour to treat with children rather than with methods and theories, and with this in mind she decided to throw more and more of the initial effort onto the children themselves.

That Harriet was well aware of the class consciousness of her day we can see in her book, and throughout the school log books; but this did not prevent her from attempting to give to the boys and girls in her care a vision of life that was considered by a few people of that era to be 'far above their station and calling'. During an evening entertainment of Morris Dancing and Folk Singing at Sompting School, a lady guest was overheard to say:

"This is all very fine, but if this sort of thing goes on, where are we going to find our servants?"

This was in 1907 and in the same year the then Vicar of Sompting wrote in the Church Magazine:

"We understand that a number of children went in for the Labour Certificate on November 9th last, but not one from Sompting. Why are the Sompting children so un-enterprising?"

Such words underline the constant friction and stress Harriet was under. The middle class worried over possible shortage of domestic labour, and the clergy did not understand why a child might want to stay on at school after the age of thirteen years.

Harriet Finlay Johnson created a climate in which the pupils would be happy, and leading from that happiness, she aroused their natural desire 'to see', 'to do' and 'to know'. They experienced learning and life that went far beyond the average reach of children who attended the usual type of school in those times. We know that she was a creative teacher and that she was 'lively' and always interested in what was happening in the world around her. Through time, she took the school, and indeed almost the whole village along with her. Her experience became their experience, her awareness, their awareness, her vision, their vision.

A test of anything that is considered to be worthwhile is the test of time. How many players in grand scenes of life live for us again through word, memory or picture, and how many are lost.

Former scholars of Sompting School, in their nineties, remember with clarity and with love, the joy of their school days. They also state specifically how fortunate they were to receive an education, which gave them a complete and thorough foundation for the life ahead. Through their testimony, Miss Finlay Johnson has presented us with living proof of the wisdom of her philosophy: happiness in learning; joy in discovery; freedom to grow; and the success of her method, education through drama.

Perhaps Mr Green, the baker in Sompting during the schools years of fame, and Mrs Bennett, the outspoken parent, are looking down in wonderment on hearing their earthly names recalled. They might puzzle at attempts to re-set the scene of their sojourn here. But in building a picture of how it was, every scrap of evidence, every incident, adds lustre to the telling. It is the words of ordinary people that touch our emotions and shape history, and it is when we can put names to faces that events become 'real'.

Vivid memories, such as the ones of the Reverend Bokenham visiting the school, holding his hands over the auburn hair of monitress Edith Riddles and saying *'I am warming them'*; of excited children crowding around Inspector Burrows to show him their latest piece of work; and later, when reluctantly he had to leave, rushing to the schoolroom window to wave to him as to a friend. Incidents that bring to life the picture of a happy, informal school, where the scholars, free to express their natural desire to learn, needed nothing of the rigid and often cruel structure of many schools at that time.

Edward Burrows, who lived in Chichester, first visited the school in April 1904. It was the start of a deep friendship, which included scholars, teachers, and finally the villagers. Intrigued by all he saw and heard, he did not confine his visits to official ones but used every possible excuse to visit the school, and there were times when scholars were invited to his home.

Nature-study, the first major innovation on the timetable, is well remembered by former pupils as being particularly enjoyable. Winter and summer alike, the Inspector would often join them for nature rambles or for lessons in the school nature garden. He was a kind hearted, caring man, with a jovial nature, rotund in build, and with a ruddy complexion. Always dressed in casual country-style clothes, his appearance belied the importance of his official position.

It was Edward Burrows who propelled the school to worldwide publicity by bringing it to the notice of the then Chief Inspector of Elementary Schools, the celebrated E.G. Holmes. And Burrows soon picked out the difficulties Harriet Finlay Johnson was trying to overcome in her work and gave her his whole-hearted support and encouragement. He demonstrated his personal interest in the revival of Morris Dances and Folk Singing in the school by attending performances in the Reading Room, the Community Hall as we know it. Interest in these activities soon expanded to include adults, and he gave great assistance to the Village Dramatic Club founded in 1906 by parents and former scholars. The ladies of the village formed a Folk Singing Group and the Inspector invited Cecil Sharpe, later known as the leading expert in Folk Singing in England, to hear them.

The glowing praise heaped on this continuation school as it was called, and the exceptional interest shown by Inspector Burrows, did not go unnoticed. The press, who were by now regular reporters on the happenings in Sompting, contributed to the overall success by adding their congratulations for what was described by some reporters as a 'return to the days of Merry England.'

A notice in the local church magazine of July 1909 informs us that:

> *"The school and villagers made a small collection to purchase wedding presents for Inspector E. Burrows on his marriage to a Miss Macdonald."*

The vicar adds a note of appreciation for the 'kindly interest Mr Burrows takes in our school and Parish.' In return, Inspector Burrows wrote two letters of thanks. One to 'My dear friends in Sompting Village', and the other, below, to 'My dear friends, the teachers and scholars of Sompting School.'

> *"Your beautiful present of a salad bowl and spoon has given me very great pleasure, and I am deeply grateful for your kind thought in sending it, and for your good wishes. That so many of you, dear children, joined in helping to make this gift adds a great deal to its value, and there is nothing among all the presents received that we care for as much as yours. Mrs Burrows wishes to send to each and all of you her heartfelt thanks.*
> *Your Sincere Friend,*
> *Edward Burrows. "*

Sadly by 1910, Edward Burrows was dead. Harriet wrote very touchingly in the preface to her book 'The Dramatic Method of Teaching' of their great loss.

"...for one who was the special friend and guardian of all our endeavours. None of the Sompting Scholars will ever forget Mr Burrows, their friend more than their Inspector!"

If Edward Burrows was friend and guardian, Miss Mary Honeywill was, to quote (more than) one source who participated in events at the time, the 'thorn in the flesh'. Born in 1868, Mary Honeywill and her sister Agatha were the daughters of a former Vicar at Sompting Parish Church, the Reverend J.B. Honeywill. The Reverend Honeywill had been Vicar at the church for many years and the school log books abound with mention of him, and frequently of his family, who also took an active part in village life.

He died in 1883. In November of that year his wife and two daughters visited the school to present the older scholars with Bibles and Prayer Books in his memory. Mary Honeywill, who was fifteen years old at the time, was given a 'very handsome Prayer Book, in affectionate remembrance of the kindly interest she has taken in the school children and their welfare.' A log book entry of that day dated November 23rd 1883 informs us that:

"as this was Mrs Honeywills last visit to the school each child received a bun'.

Mention is also made that it was Miss Honeywill's last visit, but as time would prove, this was not to be.

The Honeywills were a wealthy family and after their father's death they moved to a big house in Sompting where they had two maids and a gardener. Mary Honeywill became an influential figure in the village and the school, the log books continuing to resound to the Honeywill name. She was, among other things, the leader of the Boys Brigade, while her much quieter sister Agatha, described as being very nice, looked after the books in the Reading Room and led the Girls Friendly Society. She organised numerous events for charity, became chairwoman of the Parish Council and a manager of the school. It was common knowledge that during Harriet's time as headmistress, there was much rivalry and friction between the two ladies and that Mary Honeywill did her utmost to influence the other managers to her way of thinking.

Comments from various sources of the time ranged from 'she could make or break a teacher', 'she would stir up trouble', 'she wanted to organise everything, be in charge', 'she dominated the village'*

The arrival of the attractive Johnson sisters to Sompting must have been a difficult time for Mary Honeywill. With all the excitement, the speculation, the gossip and the new teachers at the centre of every conversation, she must have seemed 'dull'. Having lived all of her life in the village and having given her life working solely for the welfare of the villagers, she probably felt taken for granted, pushed to one side, for newcomers who had yet to prove themselves.

---

* Comments made by villagers to the author

Harriet Finlay Johnson soon proved that she had a mind of her own and would use it to make secure her potentially powerful position as headmistress. She would not be manipulated and when, for a time, she became organist and choir mistress at the church, her influence was almost limitless. The chances of two women of a similar age, both strong personalities and both struggling for power, working together successfully in a tiny village were remote. A villager, reminiscing over past times and referring to Harriet remarked *'a little diplomacy would have served'.* *

Troubles between the two may have since been understated, especially when the news broke that Harriet was to marry George Weller, a Somptingite, son of the local wheelwright and seventeen years her junior. George had been a member of Miss Honeywill's Boys Brigade, she knew his family and it was rumoured that she too had fancied him. A telling comment from one close to the scene was that *'she never forgot Harriet's marriage'.* * Most villagers, even today, remain stoical in their silence on this matter. They appear to have closed rank, and except for one or two unguarded comments, it would appear that in 1910 little was said, and no scandal attached, to a thirty-seven year old woman marrying a man seventeen years her junior.

A newspaper cutting from the *Worthing Gazette* of 1958 informs us of the passing of Miss Mary Honeywill at the age of

---

ninety years. She lived out her long life in Sompting where she spent seventy-two years as a voluntary worker for local charities. In 1948 she was awarded a long service medal with bars representing two periods of thirty years service. The daughter of a former scholar at the school who is knowledgeable about the history of the people and the place states bluntly that:

> *"Nature study was in evidence a lot... and so was Miss Honeywill".**

Another Mary, a little girl who attended the school during Harriet's day is pictured in the schoolroom giving out books from the library shelves. She attended school at the same time as the boy she later married, Nelson Hollis. Nelson particularly loved the Nature Study lessons and wrote simple poems with nature themes. He helped to build the 'Tig' shed, situated outside the school wall. He is the boy sitting on the right side of the shed roof and in the photograph of Raleigh being knighted, Nelson is standing second from the right. The children affectionately referred to Harriet as the 'governess' and late in her life Mary Hollis recalled having:

> *"...fond memories of Harriet Finlay Johnson and her sister. The 'Governess' was always so immaculate in her dress and impeccable in manners and speech. School was lovely and we had a headmistress who was so gifted but nice with it."*

---

* Comments made by villagers to the author

An example of work by Sompting pupil Nelson Hollis (see p29).

Elsie Weller, a scholar at the time and who at the age of thirteen years became Harriet's sister-in-law on her marriage to George Weller, has provided writers and historians with valuable material both from the school and as a background to village life. She used to describe her school lessons in detail to a cousin, Henry Upperton. He stayed with the family during school holidays and he remembers wishing that he had been able to go to Sompting School as it all sounded so different and exciting. When he eventually met Harriet, after she had married George, he found her to be magnetic. He described her as a 'good mixer, a great chatter-box but who never seemed to get on anyone's nerves, and a good listener too.'

Kitty and Winnie were two friends who, along with other scholars, used to stay after school to have extra tuition in cookery from Harriet and her mother. They called it a form of night school. Harriet's mother would give them tasty-bites or make tea for them in the school house when they stayed late; and they are not sure which they enjoyed most, the tuition or the tasty bites. Kitty remembers being labelled

'Kidderminster' in a geography game. Almost ninety years of age, she stated emphatically that she could not have remembered all this:

> *"… if I did not love my school life. I was sorry to leave, we were all very happy there, those were the best years of my life. We had the time of our lives."*

The two girls later became sister-in-laws, marrying two brothers from the Bashford family, also scholars at the school. One of the Bashford boys particularly, appeared to have a talent for getting into trouble. The following log book entry points to difficulties between the home and the school:

> *May 16th 1900: "Thomas Bashford, a boy in Std. 1, caught stone-throwing on his way to school, was severely cautioned by the Police Constable after morning school. The boy has been warned before and the practice seems to be spreading among the boys, therefore, all the children were warned by the Policeman. Mrs Bashford, mother of the boy mentioned, accosted the governesses on their evening walk in an insulting and abusive matter. It is difficult to expect children to maintain an attitude of proper respect to their teachers when their parents do not set them an example in this matter."*

The sombre photograph of a class drawing and painting holly for Christmas cards, taken on December 20th 1905, is the finalè of what had been a dramatic day. Having collected the holly to use in the lesson, certain scholars started throwing it around as they made their way to school. The situation became more serious when a holly berry fight erupted in the schoolroom. There was mayhem, and for years after, December 20th was known as the Day of the Big Holly Berry Fight. Order finally restored, the class involved had to stand on their forms back to back and recite mental arithmetic tables. Reciting tables is a more humane form of punishment than the one mentioned in a log book entry dated 1875:

> *"Flogged Charles Burtenshaw for climbing over the wall and opening the windows of the porches one window from the violence of the winds was broken."*

In the photograph of the class drawing and painting holly, the boy on the far left is Thomas Bashford; the boy sitting next to Thomas is sporting a black eye!

Mary Bashford vividly remembers being taken to school as an infant by her brother Tom. He had to look after her and she recalled that when he pinched apples, he would say to her over and over again, *'don't you tell mam'*. They used to take Harriet's mother, Mrs Johnson, fruit and little presents, Tom handing them to his sister to give to her between school times telling her to 'take this'. They really liked and appreciated Mrs. Johnson. Mary was forbidden to play outside after school and when she took home bits of writing for homework, her mother would say *'lot of nonsense'*.

The newspapers, both the local and the new national dailies were to play an important part in the fortunes of the school and by 1900 were already well in evidence. A heading in the Worthing paper of February 10th 1900, 'Novel Scheme at Sussex School' gives details of a scheme in which the Sompting scholars were to enter into correspondence with children of the same age in Canada. The same paper referred to the scheme again in June 1900, and wrote that the new *Daily Ex-*

press has given publicity to the idea under a double heading, 'Welding Empire', 'What a Tiny Village Does'. The article praises Harriet Finlay Johnson as a:

> *'woman with a practical, original idea for encouraging patriotism among the rising generation which is as unique as it is successful'.*

Press reports also mention her patriotic fund-raising for the widows and orphans of British Soldiers killed in the Boer War.

A year after the correspondence between scholars at Sompting and Canada started, in 1901, David Fifield from Sompting School won a medal from the Canadian Government offered by Lord Strathcona, for an essay on climate, geography and resources of Canada. David later emigrated to Australia and sadly, was killed at Gallipoli in 1915.

Harriet Finlay Johnson was aware of the power of the press. Once established at Sompting, she did not hesitate to publicise her teaching methods, and the newspapers, considering her work to be newsworthy and of value both socially and educationally, were willing to assist her. Aware of her own importance, she subscribed to a National Press Cutting Agency and diligently filled scrapbooks with relevant cuttings. Even in its infancy, one hundred years ago, the might of the press to introduce new ideas and influence public opinion marked it as a major player in promoting change, and therefore, in shaping the new world that was poised, eager to be born.

E.G. Holmes had been an Inspector for over thirty years and a Chief Inspector for two when, at the age of 57, he first visited Sompting School in 1907. A tall, handsome gentleman, always immaculately dressed, with a bearing that was 'official' but at the same time pleasant, Holmes was a conscientious, thoughtful man and a brilliant scholar. For many years he had been recognised as a leading light in the world of education, both at home and overseas, but had despaired of ever finding a school that met with his high ideals. So astounded was he by what he saw and heard over many visits to Sompting School, that he set about to try and influence a new system of education on the model of Harriet Finlay Johnson's school. He wrote a book, *What Is and What Might Be*, featuring Harriet as 'Egeria' and Sompting School as 'Utopia'. The book was acclaimed worldwide and influenced American educational practice.

On many of his visits to the school, Holmes was accompanied by Edward Burrows and other inspectors, writers and scholars. They too were similarly impressed by what they saw and heard and in turn lectured and wrote about, '*Miss Finlay Johnson's emancipation of her children in a Sussex Village School*'. One writer, in his book, *A Path to Freedom in the School*, published in 1914, states that he considers the work at Sompting School to be:

> *'One of the most interesting and convincing educational experiments ever carried out'.*

Chief Inspector Holmes wrote of Harriet Finlay Johnson's work as '*the true gospel of education*', and held it to be '*of world-wide importance and lasting value*'. It is ironic that the very man who did so much to publicise and extol her work, E.G. Holmes, also contributed to its failure to achieve permanent recognition.

Robert Morant, who was in charge of the Board of Education, appointed Holmes to be the Chief Inspector of Elementary Schools. He saw in Holmes a lively man of varied experience. Morant felt that he must have someone quick enough to apprehend what the department needed and to pass it on to the inspectorate. Morant's appointment of Holmes however, seems to have had disastrous results and was probably the cause of his (Morant's) having to leave the Board, taking Holmes with him. Morant had reigned supreme at the Board of Education for eight years when the circumstances arose which caused his resignation.

Holmes was concerned, and saw no future for education with the continuing appointment of the type of inspectors that were being promoted by the local education authorities, and in some instances, by the Board. He, Holmes, drafted a confidential report intended for the personal attention of Morant. By some curious circumstance, which has never been fully explained, the report was placed at the bottom of a pile of memoranda on Morant's desk, with the result that he signed it and thereby authorised its publication. In this report, Holmes expressed his views quite openly. He wrote:

> *"Apart from the fact that elementary school teachers are, as a rule, uncultured and imperfectly educated, and that many, if not most, of them are creatures of tradition and routine, there are special reasons why the bulk of the local inspectors in this country should be unequal to the discharge of their responsible duties'.*

The storm broke immediately the contents of the report became known. The NUT, recently formed, read the report as an unmerited attack upon the integrity of the teaching profession. A fierce battle of words, in Parliament, in the Press, and in public meetings, raged. Finally, the government saw only one option, Morant had to go, and Holmes, who was regarded as the originator of the trouble, with him.

In 1911, Harriet Finlay Johnson's book, *The Dramatic Method of Teaching* was both publicised and then overshadowed by the events of the time; events which had Holmes at their centre. His newly published book, *What Is and What Might Be*, (which had Harriet and Sompting School at its centre), drew enormous attention and the fact that he had to answer some of the criticisms that were aimed at it in another publication, 'In Defence of What Might Be', is indicative of the tremendous impact it made at the time.

That Holmes' influence in educational matters did not abate on his retirement as Chief Inspector is apparent in the many references to him in books, educational papers and journals, and in the fact that his book, 'What Is and What Might Be', has now been reproduced in five editions.

How many players in grand scenes of life live for us again through picture, memory or word:

> *"None of the Sompting Scholars will ever forget Mr Burrows, their friend more than their Inspector!"*
>
> *"Your beautiful present of a salad bowl and spoon has given me very great pleasure. That so many of you, dear children, joined in helping to make this gift adds a great deal to its value";*
>
> *"I could not have remembered all of this if I did not love my school life. We were all very happy there, we had the time of our lives."*
>
> *"Harriet Finlay Johnson's work is of world wide importance and lasting value";*

How many more are lost? It is the words of ordinary people that touch our emotions and shape history; but in building a picture of how it was, every scrap of evidence, every incident, adds lustre to the telling. Having met the cast, we can now move on to Sompting School, and to the experiment...

IV. The Sompting Experiment ~ 1897-1899

June 14th 1897	*Commenced duties as mistress of these schools today.* *H. Johnson.*

Tiny figures in groups of two and three appeared from across fields, which lay in front of the school in Loose Lane. Arrayed in all their summer splendour, the fields provided a decorative apron for the austere building. Other small figures could be seen scampering over the brow of a hill, which lay behind the school. A rough track called Church Lane led them down the hill, past Church Farm, past the Church, and on down to the road junction on West Street. From there it was a short straight walk to Sompting School.

One or two 'stragglers' emerged from a wooded plantation, which sat half way up the other side of this same hill. A small crowd strolled effortlessly along Loose Lane itself. Breaking the stillness of the morning, they pressed on to their destination. The young scholars, clutching books and parcels of food, elder brothers pulling younger, sisters coaxing infants, assembled in the girls yard. They stood quietly, expectantly, waiting for the new teachers to appear.

Harriet Finlay Johnson and her sister Emily had watched the approaching children from the schoolroom window with an air of nervousness. They knew all too well the importance of this first meeting. Rumours had spread wildly throughout the tiny community. Gossip about the arrival of the new occupants of the schoolhouse was rife. Even the tenants of the furthest farm from the village, nearly five miles away, had heard of the youthfulness and 'style' of the sisters. And this, almost from the moment they set foot over the schoolhouse threshold. It was common knowledge that their furniture included a fine walnut cottage piano that had bright red satin material ruched, and set behind a delicate fret-worked front. Lines of books, pictures, sheet music and papers were stacked – waiting their turn in the summer sunshine – for a place in the home where they would be treasured.

The children were not disappointed. Harriet and Emily walked slowly and with dignity from the schoolroom. They stood proudly in front of their wide-eyed scholars whose quiet gasps of admiration and 'faint whispers' reverberated around the yard. The teachers were even younger and more fashionable than they had imagined. As one former scholar in her nineties recalled:

> *"She [Harriet] was like a Queen. With her trim figure dressed in the latest clothes, her auburn hair coifed in the latest style, and moving so gracefully, I thought she was a Queen."*

The first flush of excitement over, Harriet raised her hand in greeting, introduced herself and Emily, then, stepping to one side, signalled to the children to enter the school. No-one moved; not a sigh nor a stirring of any kind could be heard. Then Harriet, exerting her best 'teacher voice', dramatically broke a long pause, deepening the already strained silence.

> *'Children, please march into school in an orderly manner and stand in your usual places.'*

The spell now broken, this they did.

They stood crowded together for morning prayers in a schoolroom that had been transformed beyond recognition. Even the sickly, stale smell that always greeted them on entering had gone, replaced by a sweetness and freshness that almost overpowered them as they tiptoed inside. And in their absolute quiet, the walls shouted with brightly coloured posters and pictures and cleverly contrived teaching aids. While every inch of windowsill and table top and tall teachers desk gloried in displays of wild flowers and boughs and all manner of greenery. Harriet remembered thinking that she had never been in a school where the children were so quiet.

The weeks sped by. Life in the schoolhouse settled into a calm, comfortable routine, which revolved around life in the school, with its eighty-five elder scholars, and forty-five infants. One hundred and thirty scholars taught by one teacher, one assistant teacher and two monitresses. In Harriet's first weeks we read of many distractions, which diverted her away from teaching:

> *'a.m. Vicar called'*

'p.m. Vicar called again'

'Two days holiday in commemoration of Queen Victoria's Diamond Jubilee Celebrations'

'The attendance officer, Mr Dowell, and the Vicar called'

'School Inspector called and there was a Diocesan Inspection'

'Notice of a Drawing Exam to be arranged for July'

'A visit of an Inspector for the N.S.P.C.C. (at Harriet's request made through the Vicar)

'Children taken to church for Special Feast Days'...

Looking back through the school log books a pattern emerges towards the end of the 19th century which stretches well into the 20th. A pattern of continual absence, mainly through illness or bad weather:

October 9th 1874: 'Excessive rain during the week frequently made it almost impossible for the children to get to school.'

January 19th 1877: 'The school has been half-empty this week through the children having the 'mumps'.'

June 17th 1879: 'School re-opened after a three-week closure on account of measles, the greater number of children being ill.'

November 28th 1879: 'The attendance has been very low owing to the bitter weather.'

And there were other reasons for poor attendance: minding babies, doing house-hold chores, out with mother, bird scaring in the fields for farmers, making straw bonds, not able to pay school fees: to name but a few. But when we read of official reasons why the school was closed, such as the one dated:

> *Monday October 29th 1875: 'Holiday for the purpose of making-up the accounts'*

And this after a whole week's absence due to violent storms, we begin to wonder how the children learnt anything at all!

Among numerous amusing entries is one in 1874 where we can 'feel' the despair of a teacher over the continual absence of 'girls minding babies', that she was driven to write:

> *'In this village there are multitudes of babies'.*

In 1874:

> *Friday September 18th 1874: 'A threat brought yesterday by a girl from her mother that she would be kept at home if she were forced to do lessons in the evening. Saw the mother afterwards who objected to 'home lessons' especially arithmetic. Her child could not do them. At all events not more than three evenings a week.'*

> *Friday September 25th 1874: 'Several parents still object to home lessons. One mother (whose girl has attended school exactly 54 times during the past 6 months), said these home lessons almost 'turned her brains'! and that they*

> *'paid the money' that their children might be taught at school.'*

Over twenty years later, in Harriet's time, there were still similar objections to homework and to other progressive ideas. When in 1904, her 'Dramatic Method' of teaching became a serious part of the timetable, one irate mother complained to her that she did not want her son turning 'sissy' with all those plays and new fangled ideas.

'*Next thing he'll be learning about pansies.*'

Harriet, in her spirited way replied, '*Yes, that's next week.*'

In these early days, she continued to find the children well behaved but quiet. Perhaps they were lethargic or simply bored. When all attempts to 'draw out' answers and conversations, other than the usual '*yes ma'am, no ma'am*', failed, she knew that she had to re-think her strategy. In her own words, we are told that:

> '*So little was there of initiative or originality on the part of the children themselves that I felt sure nothing short of a surgical operation, – a complete cutting away of old habits and the formation of a new school tradition, – would meet the case.*'

The first radical move away from the set curriculum of the school was made through Nature Study. Resolving that:

> '*It must not be Nature filtered through pictorial illustrations, text-books, dried specimen but must be the real study*

of living and working Nature, absorbed in the open air under conditions which allow for free movement.'

One fresh, sunny winters morning in 1897, after the assembly, which consisted of prayers, a hymn, notices and Bible reading, Harriet summoned a large group of older scholars to the schoolroom door. Excitedly, she told them they were going out onto the Downs for their Nature Study lesson. Surprised, but not so overcome that they forgot to march in the usual 'crocodile formation', the class stepped out. Once on the stony tracks however, revelling in their new-found freedom, and carried along by the enthusiasm of their teacher, they soon forgot any inhibitions. They 'sped along with the moment', joyously, naturally, as only children can.

The ramble was a success. Crocodile line disbanded, and amid all the shouting and exhilaration – part of any carefree outing – real learning took place. Huffing and puffing and ignoring the burden of cumbersome clothes, their energy knew no bounds. They jumped over sparkling streams; galloped across mounds of pungent smelling earth, and raced over short stubbly grass stopping only to collect specimens, to compare them, then search for more. Nature Study became the basis of every possible lesson. The newly cultivated school nature garden, and nature rambles, supplying subject matter for lessons in singing, reading, writing, arithmetic, drawing, composition, grammar and much of the geography.

The teachers were assisted by two monitresses; Emma Bennett and Edith Riddles, (Edith Riddles, the girl with the auburn hair mentioned earlier). In a log book entry for 1875 mention is made of 'the appointment of two monitresses, to assist teaching younger children and to sweep the schoolrooms.' Harriet valued the assistance of the monitresses as teachers. She had a strong belief in the use of 'peer' group teaching: '*Children have a wonderful faculty for teaching other children and learning from them.*' The exercise of this belief became so accepted and 'routine' at Sompting School that 'even the infants would put their hands up wanting to teach'.

Edith Riddles was the perfect monitress. Capable and willing, she shouldered her share of responsibility with a caring and seriousness that belied her young years. The children loved and respected her.

October 21st 1897

> *"Today Edith Riddles gave a lesson on pens to Std. III. Notes carefully prepared and lesson given successfully.'*

October 28th 1897

> *"Edith Riddles who has assisted in the mixed department this week, today gave a lesson on 'The Potato' to Std. III with experimental allusions to starch as formed from grated potato. Children most attentive and receptive.'*

After one particularly inspiring Nature Study lesson taken by Edith Riddles, Harriet noticed two young scholars kneeling by the edge of the garden staring at something they held in their hands. They were deeply engrossed in conversation and, on moving closer, she overheard one remark 'sternly' to the other, '*don't say dirt, say earth.*'

Despite the introduction of regular nature rambles (with permission from the Vicar and a half apology from Harriet who felt she had to explain that part of the ramble took place in the scholars' own recreation time), life within the school remained basically the same during those first months.

The year 1898 crept in with seasonal cold weather. Miss Harriet Potter joined the staff as an assistant teacher. There was the usual spate of bad attendance, illness, visits by the Vicar and a visit from Her Majesty's Inspector, T.W. Danby. Some months after his inspection, the school received a glowing government report ending with: "*This is an excellent little country school.*' And a footnote complaining that the ventilation and lighting in the boys offices was not satisfactory and the staff should be at once strengthened. The old routine of the school continued with Harriet 'daring' to alter the timetable slightly, but still adhering to a rigid curriculum, which appeared to be based on a series of object lessons.

In February and March 1898, dreadful weather continued to disrupt attendance. On March 25th a snowstorm was so severe that Miss Potter and several scholars were unable to reach the school. Those who did manage to attend were wet and cold and 'little attempt at formal lessons was made'. It was during such times that Mrs Johnson played a visible part in the chronicles of the school. She was often called upon to tend a sick child or comfort one in distress. Her caring, sympathetic nature was such that gradually over the years she made the school house a 'haven' for anyone in trouble; teacher, scholar or villager alike.

Considering they had previously lived in a densely populated area (compared to Sompting), the three Johnson ladies took to country life as if they had been born and bred there. They lived contentedly together, taking pleasure in reading, knitting, sewing and cooking, and were often to be seen walking across the Downs, even in the winter time. Villagers who passed the time of day with them on these outings gained the impression that while all three ladies were genuinely warm and friendly, Harriet had a certain aloofness about her which signalled the fact that 'she was the headmistress.' But the school, and the huge amount of work it demanded, took over the biggest part of all three lives.

By 1899 Harriet was organist and choir mistress at the Parish Church. At first enjoying the status and social acceptance such positions offered, after three years she resigned from both. Perhaps because of the enormous amount of time involved, or because of petty rivalries or jealousies, or perhaps, as has been suggested by a close relative of hers, '*she would go to church if she liked the Vicar!*'

Harriet now had the foresight to move scholars into classes or groups best suited to their needs, thus putting into practice her claim to 'deal with the child rather than the method'. The three top classes had invariably shared the main schoolroom. Now, seating changes were regularly made and there was a move away from the strict regime of 'remaining seated.' There were the usual difficulties when anything new was attempted:

February 15th 1899

> *"Mrs Dennett this week complained about her son Harold who is a most troublesome backward boy." "He has been sent to do his lessons apart and to receive special attention – which seems to have improved his lessons a little."*

February 19th 1899

> *"Mr Dennet, father of boy mentioned above, came to the school at conclusion of morning session and having enquired into the case expressed himself satisfied that the teachers were doing their best for the boy."*

– and abusive parents, something most teachers encounter sooner or later.

April 21st 1899

> *"Received rather an impudent letter from Mrs Peters, mother of a child in the infants class wrongfully accusing me of boxing her boys' ears, and implying that to be the cause of his deafness. This is totally false and is corrobo-*

rated by the whole school as witnesses. The Vicar visited this morning and I have placed the matter in his hand."

Afternoon

"The father of the child Wallis Peters came to the School at the Vicar's request and investigated the case for himself. With much difficulty he at last satisfied himself that the charge made was false and apologised."

April 24th 1899

"A written apology from Mrs Peters sent to me."

The boys in particular excelled in drawing from nature. In July the older ones took a momentous step forward when they started to use brushes and water-colours in art, on the advice of a sub-inspector, E.G. Baker, who had recently visited the school. Harriet had a natural talent for drawing, but painting was to be a new challenge for her. A challenge she relished and worked at along with the scholars, some of whom later became so expert that they won prizes for their efforts, and had work exhibited.

Devising four steps to promote original conversation and improved vocabulary, she taught them:

'How to see' (you can look without really seeing)

'To tell' (what they saw)

'Where to find their earliest impressions confirmed and crystallised' (their introduction to good literature with its (to them) new vocabulary)

'To look for reasons why'.

Months of struggle and persistence yielded results, the scholars appearing to gain new self-confidence; a self-confidence that brought with it a feeling of worthiness and an optimistic, care-free attitude to life; the dullness that had enveloped them, threatening to extinguish their natural spark, giving way to 'enquiry', 'participation', 'joy' and the sharing of their school life with Harriet Finlay Johnson as a fellow worker, playmate and friend. The relationship of teacher and scholar at Sompting School forgotten, lost forever.

The new confidence of the children showed itself in many ways. Acting on their own initiative, they took over completely the important task of collecting, arranging and the care of flowers and plants for the school. This 'duty' had started in a small, haphazard way, months earlier, in an effort to assist teachers who worked tirelessly to create an environment of interest and beauty for their scholars. Now responding, the scholars decided that a more methodical approach was needed if they were to succeed in the organisation of such an important part of school life. After much consultation among themselves, they planned a rota system. The same group of six boys and girls would be responsible for collecting, arranging and care of plants and flowers for three consecutive weeks, before handing over to the next group. Help could be sought from other scholars, and was to be encouraged, but the responsibility lay with the group in charge at any one particular time.

This 'duty' became so popular that the various groups, taking their responsibility seriously, were constantly thinking and planning ahead to when it was their turn. Even the very young ones, enthused by all the excitement, begged to join in and were often enrolled in a group as so-called 'honorary members'. Gradually the collection came to include extra specimens and an assortment of articles needed for lessons. This led to scholars becoming involved in the actual planning and preparation of lessons, which was one of Harriet Finlay Johnson's aims:

> *"I began to see how it might be possible to throw more of the actual lessons, including their preparation and arrangement onto the scholars themselves. Besides, in my opinion, more than half the benefit of the lesson lies in the act of preparing it, in hunting its materials out of hidden sources and collecting them into shape".*

The scholars roamed for countless miles searching fields and hedges, Downs and woodlands, gardens and seashore for anything of relevance; tired feet, aching legs, and hurting hands made nothing of efforts for the school and for the *governess*, as they now called Harriet, whose appreciation was unwavering. Girls could be seen hurrying along lanes leading to the school with arms full of foliage and flowers. Boys, caps perched jauntily on heads, pulling soapboxes on wheels laden with treasures lovingly collected.

They lived their school days to the full; intently, urgently, spurring each other on, charged with an enthusiasm that knew no bounds. They lived as if there were no tomorrow, and indeed for some of the young lads who forged their ages to fight and die in the Great War of 1914, there would be 'no tomorrow'. No tomorrow for them, but the eternal innocence and pure joy of gloriously happy school days where the sun shone, the birds sang, the world was exciting – and it was 'always now'.

Over the years, and until the day Harriet left Sompting School, the children never failed in the 'duty' started in 1899; and through it, they established a unique tradition, a tradition that encompassed far more than the mere collecting, arranging and care of flora.

Towards the end of 1899, Harriet found the courage to alter the timetable at will. At times the girls would be allowed to do their needlework samplers, and the boys to draw instead of copybook work. Boys would be excused a certain lesson to mend a fence, or tend to the garden; girls excused to do cookery.

During quiet lessons when the children were either drawing or sewing, Harriet played the piano for them. One of their favourite pieces was Mendelssohn's 'Spring Song' and this she played with the practice and expertise of a concert pianist. Everything she did had to be as near perfect as possible. No shoddy performance would be tolerated. She spent hours practising on her piano in the schoolhouse and would often go alone to concerts on Worthing Pier to hear the latest pop tunes of the day. Returning home she would play them for her mother and Emily, and at the earliest opportunity, give a repeat performance for the children.

The children appreciated her efforts. They learnt to listen attentively and were, in turn, inspired to aim for perfection in their own work, whatever it might be.

Her motto, *'always do your best'*, became their motto. One they took to their hearts.

In early December, the log book reports:

> *"Children drawing on slates instead of playing out in bad weather, new stencil work proceeding satisfactorily and a new system of writing by tracing with ink commenced with 'good results."*

The infants, including under fives (Harriet saw the wisdom of allowing young children into the school, thus presaging a nursery stage in education), started learning recitations and action songs for the Christmas Prize Giving. This Prize Giving was held in the school on Wednesday December 20th at 3.45 p.m. after which the school closed for the holidays.

Midnight, December 31st 1899, was perhaps the most dramatic moment in history. The passing of the 19th century; no previous century had produced as many inventions. The tremendous achievements and advances of the 19th Century heralded everything we now claim as being of the 20th. Now, the 19th century, with all its struggles and successes, was about to become 'of the past'. But with the old Queen, as ill as she was, still clinging to life, the morals and values (standards of the Victorian age), still held and would hold until she too became of the past. People tended to follow the fashion of the court; with the Queen ill, and the Boer War casting a long shadow over the country, maybe there was little mood for celebration on that last night of 1899.

In the tiny village of Sompting, sixty-six miles from the capital, there were no 'ringing of bells', symbolic or otherwise; wild jubilation's, or community activities to celebrate the approaching century. Within the four walls of the isolated schoolhouse along Loose Lane, who knows what the thoughts and feelings, regrets and reflections, of the three ladies who lived there were, at this poignant time; that no mention is made of the coming century in notes or school log books, or in any known schoolwork leading up to the end of the year is, remarkable.

Harriet, in her best 'flamboyant' style of writing, notes in the log book for the year ending 1899, "*Christmas Holidays, (school closed for two weeks)*", and that is all. Yet at the close of other years she makes special mention of what appears to be trivia in comparison to the date December 31st 1899. On one occasion she notes that it is fitting to be writing the last entry in the log book at the end of the year. On another, she comments that "*this is the last entry in the log book for this year*".

Harriet Finlay Johnson, of all people, would have reflected on the great changes that had occurred during her own lifetime. She must have dreamed dreams and had high hopes for the fast changing world of which she was a part. But her dreaming, her hoping, and her apparent lack of recognition for the significance of December 31st 1899, are pure speculation.

The fact is – however incredible it may seem that this date was 'passed over' or 'ignored' – that when Harriet Finlay Johnson opened the schoolroom door to welcome the children back after their holiday, at 8.00 a.m. on the morning of January 8th 1900, the world was in, not only a New Year, but a New Century, the Twentieth.

V. *The School Flourishes ~ 1900-1905*

> *'On cold days coal fires burned,*
> *on dark days oil lamps glowed.'*

The season of short days and long bitter nights wearied its way into January 1900. On the 8th, the school re-assembled only to close again for one more week 'owing to the prevalence of influenza.' Re-assembling on the 15th, there were still many children reported absent, owing to 'sickness and bad weather.'

Snow, blowing through strong winds, scattered, then settled on bleak Downs and stark buildings creating a romanticism lost to all but the hardiest of travellers. It was cold. The temperature of the schoolroom on one particular morning was two degrees below freezing at 9.00 a.m. rising only to 44 degrees Fahrenheit by 11.00 a.m.; cold for anyone, let alone the under fives who attended. Roaring coal fires burned determinedly throughout the building; large oil lamps, strategically placed, gave both light and heat to thankful scholars, who looked for their welcome glow as they battled their way towards the school. The comfort and welfare of children who ventured out in such fierce weather was of paramount importance to Harriet; their outdoor clothes were quickly removed and hung up to dry; damp hair allowed to tumble free was pressed with warm cloths, while hot drinks were provided from the school-house. We read of Harriet having to speak to the cleaner, 'yet again', about leaving the porch floor wet, and of her constant concern to have ample supplies of fuel and other necessary items stored, ready for harsh winters.

After the slow start to the year 1900, events at Sompting School quickly gathered pace. On February 10th, the Worthing Gazette reported that Harriet Finlay Johnson had initiated a scheme by which the senior scholars would exchange letters with children of a similar age in Canadian schools. On February 13th, Captain Dowell (the attendance Officer), visited:

> *"Captain Dowell visited and talked to the Upper Standards about their lesson which was the writing of a letter to Canada. He also brought them some foreign coins and explained their values etc."*

Replies began to arrive from Canada towards the end of the month. 'Much interest evinced and information received', Harriet noted in the log book, and a few weeks later reported that there had been a great improvement in the Composition of the Upper Classes.

On the evening of March 8th, she gave a lantern slide lecture on Canada to scholars and their parents at the school, the first evidence of her growing concern to involve parents as well as children.

In May, both the local and national press praised Harriet Finlay Johnson for the patriotic lead she took in fund raising for the widows and orphans of British soldiers killed in the Boer War. William Treagus, scholar, wrote a letter to Field Marshall Lord Roberts who was commanding the Field Forces in South Africa. The reply from Lord Roberts was framed and hung up in the school; and then, in tiny hand-writing, squeezed onto the page of the log book – as if an after thought – we read that the boy himself is to keep the original letter and a photograph of it is to be placed in the school. This same Lord Roberts was one of the last of her subjects to be received by the Queen, to hear of his victorious South African Campaign, shortly before her death.

On May 21st, there was a whole day holiday in honour of the 'Relief of Mafeking', the headmistress leading the scholars in the celebration; on the 31st, on hearing the news of the surrender of Pretoria, children 'ceased work and talked over the event'.

In the summer there were visits to Fig Gardens and Grape houses, rambles to the local chalk-pit; and object lesson rambles to learn about hills and valleys, brooks and rivers. The children wrote regularly to the local paper about their work and often had letters published. There was a visit to the local Beehives in the church grounds where the vicar gave them a lesson on Beehive management.

Out of classroom activities were now firmly established for the whole school, although there is still the stamp of formality in certain log book entries, '*Elder scholars marched to church at*

8.45 a.m.', and always the burden of rigid scripture and other examinations to prepare for. The Vicar, involved in the day to day running of the school – he signed registers and requisition forms after they had been approved by the other managers – appears to have had authority over a considerable part of the curriculum:

> *'The Vicar called and remained during the morning. He questioned Std. 111 in Geography. This class is not very intelligent but the children work to the best of their ability.'*

> *'The Vicar visited this morning and at my request cautioned a boy who had been accused of using naughty words in the street.'*

Boys were allowed to dig up part of the school grounds to plant vegetables then lettuce and other seeds, and were often to be seen in nearby fields drawing from nature. Most villagers, by now used to the sight of children wandering around during school time, note books in hand, thought nothing of it. They accepted it, and if by chance visitors to the area should 'see' and question this phenomenon, their stock answer was '*oh, its only the school.*' Parents were amused to find themselves on the receiving end of nature study lessons given by their children as they walked over the Downs; and many a picnic was arranged with a 'lesson' in mind.

While the boys were doing gardening, the girls began to have regular cookery lessons, and for their first lesson, they baked scones on the stove of the schoolhouse. By the autumn of

1900 the mention of visitors to the school is often reported in the log book:

'Boy, former scholar visited to talk to top class about his experiences in the Boer War...'

'Vicar's wife visited to see needlework to be exhibited...'

Only two of a gradual build-up of visitors throughout the year.

The new found liberalism, a move right out of conventional teaching, meant a throwing of caution to the wind, but it also meant the releasing of creative energy previously trapped inside disenchanted children, who now had the freedom to grow. Eventually, the climate of the school ignited an energy that sparked the imagination of even the weakest scholar, and willed the strongest into an ardour that could not be contained.

In a geography lesson, we read how, ' two rows of little girls with their white pinafores over their heads', represented icebergs; and of little boys who 'swam under desks', the tops of which represented ice, 'the inkwell holes were the breathing holes for the seals'. The children made a 'milk shop' in an arithmetic game, trying out the various liquid measures using 'chalky water' for milk; pounds, ounces, drams and stones presented few difficulties, with 'sea sand for sugar when dry, and when wet, cut out for butter'.

A young lad woke early to paint the sunrise out of his cottage window, anxious to capture the mood at first hand. An artist later expressed his astonishment at the immense feeling in the sky. In an article about Sompting school, the *Morning Leader* informs us that: *'The school is handsome with the pastels and water colour drawings which its tiny scholars have done.'* and the reporter mentioned his surprise on talking to a boy to find him *'troubled because in a water-colour sketch of the common Californian poppy he was painting he couldn't get the luminous quality of the yellow blossom.'*

One result of the popularity of Nature Study lessons was that children who didn't have their own plots to cultivate at home dug-up areas by the side of the road, above cart tracks, and other public places, to plant bulbs and seeds. We can imagine the amazement of the villagers as the whole area became ablaze with colourful flowers.

Little dolls were expertly dressed by the scholars:

> *'The girls frequently dressed a doll making the whole of the garment with the sewing machine – except the buttonholes – and would make it an outfit suitable for a young girl going to service, even making outdoor garments and fashionable hats.'*

Harriet continues, telling us that if she allowed them a free hand, they would make all sorts of dainty knick-knacks including *'tiny pocket handkerchiefs beautifully hemstitched with the dollies' initials worked in the corner.'*

But the pace of change had accelerated dangerously, giving plenty of ammunition to those few malcontents, (enemies) who lurked around the sidelines, watchful, ever hopeful of that one false move that could mean the end of the experiment. Meanwhile, the press continued to give publicity to the unusual 'goings on' at Sompting School and to report admiringly on the progress and the outstanding ability of its scholars.

After the Christmas holiday, the school re-opened on January 7th 1901 with three children absent. On the 10th, the Vicar called to warn of cases of Dipheria in Cokeham; the Medical Officer of Health, Dr Kelly directed that two families who attended from the Cokeham area (seven children in all), should stay at home until all cases were cleared. There were outbreaks of Scarlatina and Scarlet Fever; a young girl was sent home because of sores in her head; there were more reports of Dipheria, then measles, and through it all, the relentless winter weather to contend with.

Running parallel with the new found freedom in Sompting School was the mood of the country. Queen Victoria died on January 22nd 1901. The whole of England was plunged into mourning with everywhere silent and hushed, gloom prevailing, and all festivities postponed. On the day of the funeral, a bitterly cold day with heavy frost, the crowds, intense and silent, knew they were witnessing a historic moment. The Queen had reigned for 64 years. A great and glorious age was over and the 19th century was now truly ended.

Not surprisingly, the pomp and ceremony had hardly faded when the country turned away from the 'great and glorious' age. Released from the shackles of tight morals and stern standards of Victorian times, it looked in hope towards the light of the new century. The Victorian age had an abrupt end.

Sompting, in the midst of serious health epidemics at the time of the Queen's death, had two deaths in one week to add to its sorrow. One was the death of a boy, a scholar at the school, and the other was the death of Mrs Honeywill, the former Vicar's wife. The school closed for two separate half days as a mark of respect. Besides Harriet's beautifully written entry in the logbook:

1901, January 22nd,

'HER MAJESTY QUEEN VICTORIA (R.I.) DIED'

Other entries for that time inform us that:

January 25th : 'Service in the morning at a quarter to 9.00 o'clock for upper classes, at church.'

January 28th': All History and Reading lessons, and Object Lessons until after the funeral of our late beloved Sovereign, to bear on her life, good works, reign, and example; important changes brought about during her reign; improvements of laws; extension of Empire etc.'

February 4th': The Vicar visited and gave the children an account of the funeral of Her Late Majesty Queen Victoria (as seen by him) in London instead of the usual Arithmetic lesson.'

The following day, February 5th, the school was closed because of a severe snowstorm. We read that on the 8th, three families were still absent 'owing to Diphtheria' and that on the 14th, Standard III were given a lesson on the Union Jack.

By the year 1903, it may have seemed to casual observers that the children at Sompting were mainly engaged in cooking and gardening, now notable features of the school, or out on visits and rambles. The more formal lessons were, however, thoroughly covered, and would need to be, in order to satisfy many 'prying eyes'. Harriet had always believed that the 'informal' strengthened and gave meaning to the 'formal', although this was not easy to prove. Would-be critics were silenced for a time by a series of significant successes, which included scholars winning prizes in a spelling competition organised by a newspaper, – the prizes being presented by the Vicar; having picture essays published; a boy winning a prize at a National Exhibition for designing a Nature Calendar, and girls winning prizes for needlework.

The demands made on a head teacher, who had many masters to please at that time, were awesome. Besides regular meetings to attend and the strain of having to prepare for the frequent visits of both Governmental and Diocesan Inspections, the head teacher was responsible for all the clerical work, which included; ordering of stock, placing adverts for staff, and overseeing the maintenance of buildings, heating, lighting and cleaning.

'Must speak to the cleaner again about not sweeping the infant room.'

There were always large numbers of scholars waiting to be taught and a constant stream of visitors needing attention:

1903

September

'Meeting of Subscribers and also one of Foundation Managers in school this morning'

October 16th

'A.m. Captain Dowell and the Vicar called. P.m. Mr Watts a new attendance officer called.'

Captain Dowell, mentioned countless times in log books over the years, took a special interest in Sompting School and when he finally left in 1903, handing over to Mr Watts, his name becomes conspicuous by its absence, rather like the departing of an old friend. Poor attendance continued to be a problem for most head teachers and not only the poor attendance of scholars, as Harriet records *'The assistant teacher often absent owing to illness or bad weather or both!'*

Monitresses were also irregular in their attendance, and just as the sense of frustration over absenteeism was felt by the headmistress who wrote in 1874, *'Girls constantly absent minding babies, there are multitudes of babies in this village.'*

Harriet's frustration comes through in an entry:

November 21st 1903 'Numbers somewhat low. Newcomers to Parish do not attend so well. They find more excuses for being irregular.'

The work of Harriet Finlay Johnson was now being recognised professionally. In 1903 she was invited to become a member of the Education Advisory Committee for West Sussex County Council, and attended her first meeting at Horsham on Saturday May 16th. His Majesty's Inspector, Edward Burrows, paid his first visit to Sompting School in April 1904. The results of his visit left him 'astounded' by the high standard of the scholars work; 'amazed' at their interest, alertness and creativity; and delighted by their natural good manners and bright, happy outlook on life. After only his first visit, Harriet Finlay Johnson had acquired an influential champion, one she would later regard as 'close friend and ally'.

June 1904 saw her attending an exhibition of Nature Study at the Royal Botanic Gardens, Regent's Park, London, where some of the scholars' work was exhibited. In July of the same year, she must have felt comfortable with the idea of leaving Emily in charge of the school for three weeks as she attended a course on 'Drawing', at the School of Art, South Kensington, London. Later in the year she was the selected speaker on 'The Teaching of Nature Study in Public Elementary Schools' at a conference of Managers and Certificated Teachers. The conference was reported by the Worthing Gazette who gave a glowing account of her talk, commenting particularly on the hilarity caused by her narrative of the children planting bulbs and seeds in public areas in and around the village.

Miss Finlay Johnson had certainly 'spread her wings' since arriving at the little village of Sompting, seven years earlier. Her hectic life-style, full of excitement and diversity, now obliterated the calming silence of the schoolhouse, a silence once broken only by the sound of ticking clocks. At last, after years of anxiety, hard work, disappointments, hurts, and countless misunderstandings, things were going her way. She did not know, at this point in time, that through the chance remark of a child, she was about to embark on the most controversial and far-reaching of all her methods, 'The Dramatic Method of Teaching'.

It was a cold, wet day in the Autumn of 1904. The children, not able to play outdoors, had to content themselves with reading or playing indoor games during their break times, but the dark, heavy clouds, producing thoroughly miserable weather, couldn't penetrate the walls of the schoolroom or dull the cheerful scene inside.

A history lesson was taking place. The Upper Classes had been reading Sir Walter Scott's 'Ivanhoe' as an adjunct to the study of the reign of Richard the Lion Heart and his times. A talk by Harriet and a discussion with the children of the characters in the book led to remarks from the boys such as, '*If I had been so and so I should have done so and so…*' As play out of doors was impossible, someone suggested, '*Couldn't we play*

'Ivanhoe' indoors?' No time was wasted in arranging scenes and casting parts. From that moment, Harriet had no doubt as to whether a play in school could be successfully managed.

> *'First arouse the desire to know', one of the first essentials in teaching.'*

Boys settled on a rosy, rotund boy for a jovial Friar Tuck, who at once placed himself under a high spindle-legged desk which he called his hermits cell. *'I'm the Black Knight'*, said another, dragging his black jersey over his head for a suit of chain mail. Soon the play was in full swing and the schoolroom became anything or anywhere their imagination desired.

After the initial performance of scenes from 'Ivanhoe', they began to study the book more closely for dialogue, understanding and searching for meanings and allusions, some of which the elder scholars quickly learned to find in the dictionary.

> *'Here then was English studied voluntarily. An enormous amount of general knowledge can be acquired in the hunt for meanings and derivations of words.'*

Harriet found that the scholars gathered a new huge vocabulary, 'Each subsequent performance of scenes from Ivanhoe showed a marvellous improvement in knowledge and intelligence and they used the text book in its proper place, not as the principal means, but merely as a reference for assistance.' The Grand Master in the story led to the children asking what he was 'Grand Master' of, which led to a deeper study of local history and to the connection long ago between the 'Order of Knights Templar' and their own village church.

A wonderful resourcefulness was shown in getting over difficulties in the play, and Harriet was delighted to find that there was always one or another who would come forward to do the necessary work. Scholars themselves suggested costumes and properties, some of which the girls made out of silver paper tea wrappings from home. One morning a boy brought a set of horse brasses into the playground to decorate the war-horse used in the play. Children crowded around to see them and excitedly trooped into school to show their treasures to the teachers.

The overall success of this first venture into drama as a means of teaching history, opened the door to radical changes throughout the curriculum. Young scholars, Harriet believed, would learn if and when they wanted to learn, and she discovered that a desire for knowledge can be aroused by dramatisation.

> *'When our scholars began to dramatise their lessons they at once developed a keen desire to know many things.'*

The first plays were adapted plays arranged from historical novels and reference books, (no play was adapted from any one book), the books placed within easy reach of the children. The boys erected four long shelves made out of disused gallery desks in a corner of the schoolroom; this became known as the library corner. Scholars could be found there, either before, during, or after school time, studying books, making notes, or holding quiet discussions about the work in hand. The library books included, as well as historical novels, one serious study of each reign or period of English history, and 'True Stories of British History'. 'True Stories of British History' was a firm favourite.

'Children prefer stories that are true and will go to great lengths to re-create the appropriate environment.'

Realism in the plays was portrayed in a number of ingenious ways. During one battle scene, 'Girls simulated the rattling of musketry by throwing fresh laurel leaves on the schoolroom fire where they crackled, sputtered and smoked.' Big brothers and fathers became interested, and properties began to come in. One father made a brass crown inset with coloured glass jewels; another made a heads-mans axe; several people presented the school with wooden swords, the blades silvered; an elder brother carved daggers which had bloodstained points. Boys were allowed to ride their soapboxes – those with guiding wheels in front – to re-enact a grand sea fight between the Dutch and the English. Queen and court ladies robes were fashioned from white lace window curtains, pinned at the shoulders, and allowed to trail.

'The change in deportment of both boys and girls as they stepped into various roles was remarkable.'

Queen Elizabeth's state barge was a soapbox draped in red cloth. Charles escaped to France in a disused hip bath which,

Harriet tells us, 'rocked beautifully'. From the same bath, fishermen on the Volga hooked giant fish in the shape of the school dusters. She found the most comical properties to be a set of brown paper animal skins into which small boys would creep, adding a realistic touch to geography and other plays. Mike, a highly talented young man and a natural leader, designed and painted the costumes; the girls sewed them up. In Mike, Harriet found a bold spirit who, in other less challenging circumstances, might have become bored and 'warped into a ring leader or troublesome scholar'. Now, with the system of 'freedom with discipline' well established, and the trust between all parties secure, Harriet only had to say '*Mike, suppose you take the books and go to the top of the playground, choose your parts and try what sort of a play you can make from what you have collected*', and in no time at all it was done.

But the drama, with all its ingenious props and costumes and scenery was not devised to be acted in front of an audience. There were no 'stars', and the roles were interchangeable. Every child had some part to play in the proceedings, which included, doing the research, writing out parts; in the chorus, acting as crew or citizens; making notes as an observer, making props or costumes, stage managing, and all were equally important:

> *'I soon found that I could throw more and more of the work onto the children themselves. They became self-reliant, mainly self-taught, and developed a habitual thoroughness in all they attempted.'*

Inevitably, the happiness and excitement of life at Sompting School continued to infiltrate the village and surrounding area to the extent that by 1905, villagers were not surprised at anything. If they saw a Knight in shining armour ambling along a lane, a soapbox with a drainpipe fixed to it for use as a canon being pulled by soldiers of another age, fairies appearing from out of the woodland, it didn't matter, no questions were asked, it was only the school.

The year 1905 disappeared even quicker than the previous year. Nature study lessons continued to blossom and grow, there were the usual rambles to the seashore or across the Downs; plays were acted on the Downs or under the Elm tree in the school grounds; the Vicar continued his almost daily visits, on one occasion calling to discuss the question of 'teaching cottage gardening and cookery'. Log books inform us of examinations to prepare for; a history game being played during a history lesson; pancakes made on Shrove Tuesday; saluting the flag and singing the national Anthem at the start of school on May 24th, Empire Day, and various experiments - including one on air pressure – being attempted. Harriet was now frequently absent to attend meetings of the Advisory Committee at Chichester, but such was the order of the school that, when necessary, scholars could be left to work unaided, with only the assistant teachers and monitresses nearby.

The time for fires to be lit came round again and the time for yet another reading of Dickens' 'Christmas Carol', sitting comfortably in front of a 'rosy glow'.

> *'On dull, dreary, wet winter afternoons we would revel in the spirit of good humour and loving kindness which Dickens designs to inculcate. How magically he constructs an atmosphere.'*

In their enthusiasm for the story the scholars devised scenes from its pages and acted them during playtimes and after school.

> *'I feel convinced that the mere act of playing and enjoying the 'Christmas Carol' was a true education to my scholars. Who, at Sompting School will ever forget watching the elder boys and girls as they acted the 'Cratchits Christmas Dinner', entering most wholeheartedly into the spirit of the thing.'*

Through the play they had the opportunity to show how sensitive they were to the feelings and needs of others; to portray concern as they 'worried' about the boy who was suspected of not having enough to eat; express sympathy for the girl who had her ears boxed by her mistress; sadness for the poor, the sick, the lonely. And through the play, in quick response to changes of mood, they could soar to glorious heights of exhilaration, laughing hilariously as they romped through the Fezziwigs Ball dancing the Sir Roger de Coverly as if their very lives depended on it! Advance and retire, hold hands with your partner, bow and curtsey, corkscrew, thread-the-needle and back to your places…

'We all had such a bright time.'

Contrasting to the joy Harriet found in working with the children was the irksome fact of life in the real world, where there were always parents to appease; the need for constant diplomacy in the face of what was, at times, sheer ignorance on the part of officials and other critics; and the continual disruption to school work, which included the Annual Clothes Distribution day. This event, organised by Miss Honeywill, was held only one week before the Christmas Holiday. Harriet and Mary Honeywill often met through school or church affairs, the 'aloofness', the frosty politeness' between them causing embarrassment to others, who were made to feel uncomfortable in their presence. Many 'frownings, tut-tutts and snide remarks' had to be ignored by Harriet as she pressed on with her ambitious plans for the school. Try as she might, Mary Honeywill had not as yet persuaded the managers to curtail her grand schemes, but Harriet was aware that she had to tread warily in her bold endeavours.

On November 9th, she received the report of the Diocesan inspection which had been held on the 7th; breathing a heart-felt sigh of relief as she scanned the list of tests to find them all marked 'excellent', except for one which was in any case, marked 'very good'. She was particularly pleased with the Inspectors' concluding remarks, the last sentence of which states:

> *'The discipline of the school is excellent and the tone is quiet and reverent.'*

On the last day of term, December 22nd 1905, Harriet made the final entry of the year in the log book, 'Closed school for the Christmas holidays this afternoon. The children performed a play, 'The Christmas Carol.'

While it snowed, the snow turned to rain, and a bitter wind swept howling over the Downs.

Sompting girls prepare Christmas puddings under the watchful eye of Emily Finlay Johnson.

VI. *A Growing Reputation ~ 1906-1909*

It was a well kept secret, and in a village the size of Sompting, where everybody knew everybody else and everybody else's business, a secret was a miracle; however, in July of 1906, Harriet Finlay Johnson applied for another position in a school in Surrey. This revelation, only recently made public by present day researchers, caused much consternation to those left who had known her, particularly her former pupil and sister-in-law Elsie Weller.

The question, 'why would she want to leave', has been posed many times. Her own reason appears to be that she felt she had too many masters to please at Sompting School, and wanted to 'work in a Council School under one authority.' It is only after studying her private papers and assimilating the evidence they produce that we realise the depth of animosity felt towards her (particularly from one quarter), and the determination to curtail her activities.

Leading up to what was a major decision for a woman in those days (her mother and Emily would also be seriously affected by any move she made) were a series of incidents starting in January 1906; perhaps the most important one being the removal of the school piano, a well calculated, under-hand blow. Harriet couldn't even bring herself to record the removal in the log book at the time, but mentions it in a rather 'casual' way a week later:

> *'Requisition received, four books disallowed, school piano removed last week'.*

A confusing account of why it was removed appears to give the reason as the extra cost incurred on the Insurance Policy. The school however, had always housed a keyboard instrument; as far back as 1872 we read in the log book of a 'new American organ' being purchased. In March 1906 she received notice that 'no under fives' were to be admitted unless by special arrangement with the Local Authority; yet another interference in a policy she firmly believed in and had successfully implemented.

Meanwhile, the school's fine and growing reputation for Nature Study encouraged many visitors. During the first half of 1906 no fewer that four of 'His Majesty's Inspectors' visited, one returning a second time solely to see the methods used in the teaching of this subject. Harriet continued to work with three large classes, helped by an assistant teacher (there were now two assistant teachers and Emily); to attend regular meetings of the School Advisory Committee; to prepare for the yearly Dicoesan Inspection – from which an excellent report was received – and to oversee the 'care' of the building.

> *'Sweeping of Infant room (Monday morning) very unsatisfactory. Little heaps of road-dirt beside all the iron standards of the desks.'*

There were the usual spates of inclement weather, and in March no less than nine scholars were absent with 'bad throats'.

True to her commitment to community involvement Harriet continued to encourage parents to partake in school life; she organised adult groups – with the unstinting help of Inspector Burrows – in drama, folk-singing, music and Morris dancing. The 'show-case' for these groups to perform, along with scholars, was the annual concert in the Reading Room, again organised by Harriet Finlay Johnson.

Whatever happened in July 1906 to change her mind – having applied to leave the school at the beginning of the month and to stay by the end of it – is left to speculation. But, armed with a new zeal and determination to succeed, Harriet put all thoughts of leaving Sompting behind her. Building on the hard won foundation of previous years, and burning her boats behind her, she set out to prove her theories in no uncertain terms. Now disdainful of the previously felt need to be constantly 'looking over her shoulder', and of having to ask permission for every paltry change she wanted to make, she strode boldly forward; fired with the conviction of her beliefs and unshakeable in the proven success of her methods.

The autumn term of 1906 saw many changes to the timetable, including the first serious mention of 'correlated lessons'. On September 25th, three Governesses and four students from 'Bishop Otter College', Chichester, spent the morning hearing a nature lesson with some elder scholars and *'One of the new 'correlated' spelling, drawing and writing lessons with std I and II'*. Boys were allowed time (instead of a composition lesson) to make a fence to put round the playground garden; and we glimpse the depth of Harriet's understanding of children and her sincerity in working with them when we read that, one week later, they are given another 'free' lesson in Composition time to complete their garden fence, *'this in order to supplement their own efforts in their playtime.'*

We can almost 'hear' their plea for one more free lesson in order to finish the fence, 'we did most of it in our own time ma'am'.

Miss Pullen Burry, a member of the British Association, called one afternoon *'and related to children some accounts of her travels in British Colonies'*.

Mr F. Witcomb, local West Sussex County Council Inspector often visited. Miss Moseley, 'Physical Inspectress' visited, and possibly because of her visit the elder boys were allowed '10 minutes in addition to their usual playtime', for organised football during the last lesson on a Friday afternoon.

One afternoon in October 1906, the 1st. class boys started organised football first lesson instead of last, as the cows would occupy their field during last lesson. Harriet informs us that she is trying the experiment of organised games before finally altering the timetable.

Inspector Burrows, usually accompanied by a number of guests, continued his regular visits and enjoyed watching the history plays. In November, the Reverend H.S. Norden, a new Vicar, called for the first time.

We read of 'organised games on nature work, geography etc. for Std. I and II', the word 'games' meaning the drama or 'play' and of 'elder boys planting wheat in the playground garden, their first experiment in farming'. On December 7th 1906, Mr. and Mrs Norden called and asked Harriet to give out tickets for the Annual Distribution of Clothing to be held in the school on the 14th.

On the 10th of December 1906, a representative of the Morning Leader – and within a few days two reporters from National Dailies visited. The National Dailies published double-page feature articles with photographs of scholars 'acting their lessons' and one of Emily and a group of girls making plum puddings for Christmas. Local and National press reports and visitors – many of them influential – continued to keep Harriet Finlay Johnson, the school, and the village, in the public eye not only in England, but in places as far away as America and Japan. The term ended quietly on the 20th of December, the day before the publication of the feature article in the 'Daily Mirror' and recommenced on January 7th

1907, four days after the publication of a feature article in the 'Daily Mail'.

Having been featured in both local and National press during the holiday, and no doubt basking in the limelight and accolades such publicity would bring, it must have been a humbling start to the year 1907 for Harriet to find that on the first morning back;

> *Jan. 7th The attendance officer called and investigated the cases Peters (Ringworm) and Smith.'*
>
> *On the 9th 'School porch very soppy with water this morning. The cleaner left it without attempting to dry it.'*

and a slow start to the year as we read;

> *Jan. 22nd 'The weather is very severe and the attendance is suffering much from that and from Influenza.'*

By the end of January both scholars and teachers were suffering from Influenza and although, in February, some semblance of normality was attempted –

> *Feb. 6th '1st. class sent for a nature ramble this afternoon instead of gardening (for boys) and drawing (for girls).*
>
> *Feb. 12th 'Elder girls made pancakes this afternoon (Shrove Tuesday).'*

By the 21st of February there is some concern over cases of Whooping Cough in the Infant's Department.

25th. Feb. 'School closed this afternoon by certificate from Dr Millbank-Smith in consequence of Whooping Cough.

THREE WEEKS CLOSED.'

18th. March 'Reopened school. 14 Infants still ill; 8 elder scholars. Dr Millbank-Smith called after morning session and advised the exclusion of 4 additional Infants and 5 elder scholars in whose houses Whooping Cough is still present. The Managers called and Attendance officer wrote that he could not be present.'

20th March 'Head teacher attended meeting of Advisory Committee at

(Wed.) Horsham this afternoon.'

28th. March 'School closed for Easter Holidays.'

19th. April 'Extension of holiday for another week in consequence of Whooping Cough.'

Although children were still absent at the end of April with Whooping Cough, things were starting to look brighter. On May 1st 1907 we read of a half-day holiday to gather flowers for the usual May day celebrations, and visitors to the school were in evidence again, observing scholars at their lessons. On May 15th, the elder boys went out sketching to the sea front, and on the 17th the school closed for the Whitsun holidays, (one week).

The eagerly awaited days of summer arrived at last and in their first flush held the promise of gloriously hot months to come.

Lessons often took place outdoors, under the shade of the Elm tree which stood by the path in front of the school, or on the Downs. Visitors could find themselves listening to a singing lesson, or watching a history play, in the little wooded plantation that lay between the school and the old church; or visiting the 'Tig' shed built by the boys. This 'shed' was used as an excellent base for playing 'Pre-historic Times'; for making pottery from local clay (cups and basins made here were added to the school museum started by Harriet some years earlier), and for the manufacture of ancient weapons and cookery. The scholars smoked a herring, and one unfortunate guest, invited to sample the remains, did so with 'good grace', whatever his private doubts may have been.

Outings were whole afternoons and took in any manner of lessons that led from one discovery to another. There was a whole day's outing to London where the children had a trip on the new London County Council river steamers from Westminster to the Tower. They were impressed by the offices of the Board of Education and wished they could have heard a debate in the House of Commons, and they explored nearby slums. As Harriet tells us, after seeing the '*great unwashed*', they wondered to see a sign at a street corner;

> '*Wash and brush up, hair cut & shave, etc.*'

One boy said '*why don't they come here if they are so dirty?*' Best of all, they enjoyed their visit to 'The National Gallery' and finally a visit to 'Madame Tussaud's.'

A friend of the school presented copies of 'Wood Magic and 'Bevis' by Richard Jefferies. *'Tales of human children'*, Harriet comments, *'and therefore they appealed to human children.'* In her book she writes:

> *'In the story of Bevis we have an account of how two school boys 'played' school; how they manufactured a gun, a raft, a boat and went on a voyage of discovery round a small lake, finding a real island and living on it.'*

She continues, explaining how much the children, and herself, were *'fired'* with enthusiasm to *'play'* it:

> *'Our boys, on reading it, were instantly fired with the desire to play it. I must confess, so likewise was I. Bevis's first craft was an old wooden packing-case and his scene of operations a brook near his house. Very good packing-cases we had in plenty in the school shed, and a brook within ten minutes of the schoolhouse. The packing-cases were heavy, and July days are often hot, but down to the brook we hied us on the hottest day I have ever experienced. The air quivered with heat, and not the slightest particle of shade could we find – not even a hawthorn-bush. But the spirit of adventure was upon us and would not be quenched.'*

Her description goes on to include; 'A *network of brooks and drains, wooden bridges for cattle to cross from one pasture to another*'; and then describes how the group finally settled on one of the bridges for '*Our base of operations.*' Harriet observes that '*Bridges have always a fascination for children.*'

> '*Naturally we had to experiment a good deal before the packing-case behaved itself properly as a raft, but when it did and the first passenger gently punted under the bridge, excitement ran high. Soon off came boots and stockings and we were all in the thick of a game.*'

On reading this account of the 'outing' it is interesting to ponder over the obvious relationship of complete trust which must have existed between the teacher and the scholars before such an experiment as '*riding on a raft under a bridge*', could take place.

Employers were now seeking to engage children from the school, so impressed were they by the character of former scholars and by the quality of work they produced. They were found to be conscientious, self-reliant, cheerful and contented, qualities Harriet Finlay Johnson sought to foster in their education.

She tells us in her book about the girl who first impersonated Rebecca in the history play 'Ivanhoe' finding employment as a general servant in a clergyman's family. The girl was so bright and contented that everyone remarked what a contrast she was to the ordinary 'girl-of-all-work.'

> '*Moreover, her employers found her so well-informed and so well able to impart to others what she knew, that they allowed her to assist the young daughters of the house with*

their home studies in the evening. She did this quite naturally – with neither false humility nor swelled head. She was evidently able to adapt herself to any circumstances.'

This was not an isolated case, for Harriet continues:

'All the little girls who have gone out to service from the school have been of the same calibre.'

One boy, who became the manager of a large store in Sussex, accredited his happy and successful life to the education he had received with Harriet Finlay Johnson. He never tired of praising her or her methods, and particularly remembered asking her if he could recite 'The Charge of the Light Brigade', by Tennyson. At the end of the poem,

'Honour the charge they made,

Honour the Light Brigade,

Noble six hundred'.

The boys added a realistic touch by having a Roll Call of supposed survivors, the last man staggering up just as his number was called, answering his name, then falling down dead. The boy, who lived well into his nineties, continued to recite the poem throughout his life, no doubt remembering his school pals when he came to the last verse, the power of the words invoking ghostly echoes of voices long since silent.

Mabel Kennard was a girl who, encouraged by Harriet, applied for a job at the new telephone exchange opened in

London. This was a daring and unusual thing for a girl to do at that time, but she was successful in her application, and spent many happy years working there. The girls, well used to making cakes or 'dainties' for plays, concerts, and Infant tea parties, wanted something more elaborate to use as a wedding cake. After school one evening, in the schoolhouse, Harriet set about showing them how to ice a cake, and allowed them to assist her. One of the group was so interested that she practised it over and over again at home and less than a year later won a prize for an iced cake in a county competition. A few years later she made and iced her own wedding cake.

Educational visits continued, including one to watch a kite-flying demonstration on a nearby hill, and another to see a newspaper printed with the new machinery at Worthing. Captain Dowell's name appears again in the log book, informing us of a visit he made with a Colonel Pierson to see a history play. A reporter from the Daily Mail tried to engage Harriet in a discussion about the difficulties she had encountered in trying to establish her methods, but she would not be drawn, she simply tossed her head back and said, laughingly, '*Oh I please myself now.*' After school activities, including concerts, folk-festivals, competitions, clubs (the mothers now wrote and produced their own plays), lessons, visits, happy days, with school and home life in the village of Sompting blurring into one long, continual 'happening'. Only the changing seasons marked the passage of time for Somptingites completely absorbed in a medley of life that took them above the mundane, onto a higher level of experience.

As summer in all its glory presaged the rich colours of autumn, thrilling and inspiring yet further those souls awakened to the beauties of nature; as cold winds blew the winter in with icy breath and violent gusts, suddenly, it was November the 26th 1907; the fateful day on which His Majesty's Chief Inspector of Schools, E.G. Holmes visited Sompting School for the first time.

> *Nov.26th E.H. Burrows Esq. Brought E.G.A. Holmes (H.M. Chief I.) to spend the whole day at the school.'*

Harriet's modest entry in the log book recording the Chief Inspector's first visit, belies the tremendous impact that first visit made on him.

> *'It was in November of the year 1907 that I paid my first visit to Sompting School, the first of many visits. That visit made me an ardent Somptingite and set me thinking about education as I had never thought before.'*

In over thirty years as an Inspector, Holmes had failed to find his ideal school, and had despaired of ever finding it. In the morass that was the education system, with children sitting in long rows, in large dreary rooms, taught by teachers with a narrow outlook, using mechanical methods of teaching; scholars not allowed to think for themselves; fed fact after fact without any thought given to meaning or understanding; and because of the inadequacies of an education system which conspired to prevent the growth and development of the child, leaving him with low intellectual expectations – Holmes had lost faith in the potential of the average child and man. He felt that there was no hope, no prospect of improvement; and it was here that Sompting School was to prove him wrong and give him a new fervour for education, and a rekindled faith in mankind.

Two weeks later, on the 11th. December he returned to the school.

> *Dec.11th E.G. Holmes Esq. (H.M. Chief I.) visited all day and watched the working of the school.*

and again the following day;

> *Dec. 12th Mr. Holmes again visited. He was accompanied by B. Hawker Esq. and both remained for the evening performance (by the scholars) of Morris Dancing and folk singing. Both expressed themselves more than highly pleased by the novel and effective methods employed throughout the school and were surprised by the results.*

Holmes tells us how each succeeding visit deepened his interest in the school and heightened his appreciation of it. Soon he was writing of scholars whose personal growth and development exceeded any of his early expectations; expectations he had held before becoming disillusioned with the whole process of education.

'Activity, versatility, imaginative, sympathy, a wide and free outlook, self-forgetfulness, charm of manner, joy of heart, these are the qualities which flourish in the soil and atmosphere of Sompting School. They are the outcome of a type of education which differs radically from that which has hitherto been accepted as orthodox.'

Words that resonated world wide, giving major publicity to the school. The writer R.J.W. Seleck informs us that Harriet Finlay Johnson's school so shocked Holmes that he:

'Attempted to get to the bed-rock of her philosophy of education'. When he had finished this task he found that the obscure Sussex school had led him not just to an attack on the methods of elementary education but to a criticism of the entire educational system and indeed, of Western civilisation."[1]

And in referring to the book by Holmes 'What Is and What Might Be', published in 1911, in which Holmes extols the work of Harriet Finlay Johnson as the 'True gospel of education; Selleck continues:

'Holmes was to become an important reformer in his own right, but had he done no more than describe Harriet Finlay Johnson's school he would have left his mark!'

[1] R.J.W. Selleck – 'English Primary Education and the Progressives 1914-1939.'

Following the publication of 'What Is and What Might Be', Holmes became recognised as the key figure in the New Education which became labelled the 'Progressive Movement'; and Harriet Finlay Johnson became recognised as the inspiration for the 'Progressive Movement', both here and in America.

Between March 1901 and March 1910 there were no less than forty-eight visits of Inspectors, most of them His Majesty's Inspectors and from places as far apart as Cumberland, Staffordshire and Norfolk; but 1908 was the 'peak' year for visitors; and leading the way was the Chief Inspector himself, Edmond Holmes. Inspector Holmes often visited on consecutive days, invariably accompanying the children on their rambles. Walking with a girl who had recently moved to a village over three miles away, and yet who continued to attend her old school with 'faultless regularity', he asked her what she would do if her home was six miles away. She answered without a moment's hesitation, *'I'd come just the same.'*

> *Jan. 15th 1908'Inspector Witcomb visited & told the Head teacher that it was desired by Board of Education that an exhibit of scholars' work be sent from this School to Tokyo, Japan.'*

We read of the children working hard preparing material for the exhibition (which was to be a permanent one) and finally putting forward forty-three items. On July 4th the popular women's weekly 'Home Chat' published a long, special feature article with photographs on the school. The reporter wrote of feeling fascinated and uplifted by his visit. Later in the year a Diocesan Inspection resulted in yet another excellent report, the last line of which reads, '*The tone of the school is admirable.*' As many children as possible were taught the elementary rudiments of gardening and eventually a large vegetable garden, formed within the school grounds, became well known for the excellence and variety of its produce. The children's efforts at drawing and painting were earning praise and publicity. Inspector Burrows, accompanied by His Majesty's Inspector, Mr H. Tunaley – Chief Inspector of Drawing, under the Board of Education – arrived to inspect the art. Mr Tunaley submitted an informal report to Inspector Holmes;

> '*In this school the teaching of Drawing reaches the highest educational level I have hitherto met within our elementary schools, and the results are the genuine expression of the children's own thoughts.*'

But the constant stream of visitors, particularly so many from the Senior Inspectorate, and the strain of being almost permanently in the public eye, must have taken its toll, especially on the assistant teachers. Harriet and Emily would be sustained by the success and excitement of it all; the monitresses would enjoy the attention; but the assistant teachers, there were now two, (if they were not fully behind the "new education"), must have been bewildered and perhaps even traumatised by the whole experience. Children would soon sense if a teacher was not "in tune" with the school, (one was given the name "muggy tea-leaves"). In April 1908 an effort to recruit a new teacher to replace one who had recently left, caused some confusion, according to the log books;

April 9th	*'The Vicar visited this afternoon and instructed me to insert advertisement in order to fill vacancy which will occur in staff in consequence of the resignation of Miss Skinner.'*
April 10th	*The advertisement referred to has not been inserted as there are some applicants for the post.'*
15th	*'School closed for Easter Holidays. Two weeks. (longer because of whitewashers and painters)'*
May 4th	*'School reassembled. Miss Keys and Christiana Downey at work temporarily as staff. Advert. Inserted in School-Master for permanent help, since none has been appointed.'*
11th	*'Two candidates interviewed for post of Supplementary Teacher today.'*
16th	*'Managers meeting to appoint staff.'*

Miss Grace Dora Godball was appointed as Supplementary Teacher on June 1st. Subsequent log book entries for the rest of the month reveal the relentless pressure staff were under;

June 2nd	*'Mr Kenny Herbert (His Majesty's Inspector) with three Junior Inspectors visited all day.'*

3rd. *'The above gentlemen again visited during morning session.'*

5th. *'Mr Watson & party (Petworth) visited all day.'*

11th. *'Miss Robinson & niece (Barnham) visited all day'*

15th. *'Mr Watts visited.'*

19th. *'The scholars are preparing an exhibit for the Chichester Agricultural Show.'*

26th. *'Mr Carter (Board of Education) visited all day.'*

and they were often absent for one reason or another;

October 2nd. *'Miss Godball sent home. Her father is dying.'*

12th. *'Miss Godball returned to her duties.'*

17th. *'Miss Keyes absent with sprained foot.'*

20th. *'Miss Keyes still absent.'*

26th. *Miss Keyes still absent. Certified by doctor. Miss Godball had to go home this afternoon also with a sprained foot.'*

The weather continued to be a favourite source of conversation in its unpredictability – partly as a consequence of which the usual illnesses were never far away;

'Two children, suspected of Whooping Cough, sent home. This is the third case since August holidays.'

And there were the usual health and behavioural problems;

> *November. 'Two boys, James & Edward Allen, taken by Infant mistress to the Vicar (as Chairman of the Managers) because they are sent to school in a dirty condition. Also their mother sent note, couched in impudent terms, relating to the fact that the boys are not allowed to remain at school during dinner hour owing to their pilfering habits. This afternoon the boys have returned to school slightly cleaner.'*

On one occasion, one of the assistant teachers had to go to hospital; another had to take her there, the third was ill in bed and Harriet was detained by one of the managers on her way to school for over half an hour. When she finally did arrive, she found all the children in their places, hard at work. They had looked at the timetable, chosen some of the older scholars to teach the lower classes, and then settled down '*happily and in perfect order*'.

In November, 1908, Mr Frank Benson, the great Shakespearean actor, performed Julius Caesar at the Theatre Royal, Worthing. Harriet already had links with him and his company, which included the well-known Shakespearean actress, Estelle Stead, daughter of W.T. Stead, social reformer and editor of the *Pall Mall Gazette*, who died when the *SS Titanic* sank in 1912,

Harriet and Estelle were close friends and when Harriet took a party of scholars to see the play at the Theatre Royal, they were all invited backstage after the performance.

The young men of the village, many of them former scholars at Sompting School, asked Harriet to help them start a drama club. Named the "Men's Dramatic Club", it was formed in the autumn of 1908 and met three evenings a week in the schoolroom. Inspired and encouraged by Frank Benson – who visited the school on a number of occasions – the men decided to produce the play "Julius Caesar" with the omission of Act One and scene 2 of Act 2. Rehearsals went ahead with all the fervour and seriousness of a dedicated professional company; the men studying the script and reading histories to ensure that they had the correct interpretation of the parts and that the properties were accurate. Mr Burrows, who had helped Harriet with the founding of the club, was closely involved, and at a later stage in the proceedings, Frank Benson again visited and watched a rehearsal. He was suitably impressed, commenting especially on the clever casting of parts.

The venue for the "Men's Dramatic Club" production of Julius Caesar was to be no less a place than the Theatre Royal, Worthing, and by Christmas 1908 anticipation in the village ran high when the date for the performance was announced as February 16th 1909.

The local newspaper followed the rehearsals with interest and gave regular reports on the progress of the play. It was reported that on one, wet Saturday, the men spent '*eight consecutive hours (with a short interval for tea!) in practising with their Roman costumes on*', and as the day of the performance neared, one reporter wrote amusingly of the young men's dismay (there were eighteen with speaking parts and their ages ranged from sixteen to fifty two) at having to sacrifice their whiskers '*to the art.*' The reporter continued:

> '*the men are so involved in the play that when you see a man turning over a manure heap beyond the hedge as you pass along, he will gravely give you a 'Roman Salute.*"

At the beginning of February the men in the dramatic club travelled to London to see Frank Benson and his company perform Henry the V at the Coronet Theatre. Once again they were encouraged and inspired by the famous man, and at a crucial time, their own performance being imminent. He apologised that neither himself nor his wife would be free to attend their performance at the Worthing Theatre Royal, but later sent a telegram of congratulations and best wishes to all involved in the production.

Monday evening, the 15th of February 1909, and the night of the dress rehearsal. Estelle Stead, who had agreed to be the stage manager, arrived at the theatre early, ready to give her professional help and support; Mr Burrows, ever present, assisted, and was warmly thanked by all the participants for the expertise, the time, and the friendship, he so freely gave; and Harriet, lauded as the producer, spoke of suddenly feeling an inward "humility" and "awe", as she stared around her, seeing happy, yet anxious faces, and realised for the first time the enormity of the undertaking. On the 16th February, the big day, Sompting School had a holiday. Almost the whole village was on holiday, except for those who had to tend to the animals, and by six o'clock there was a mass exodus from the area as people made their way on foot, by pony and trap, or bicycle, to Lancing or Shoreham Stations, where special trains were waiting. The cost of the venture, which included the hiring of costumes, theatre, and theatre orchestra (to play the incidental music) was covered by a "packed house" paying "nine-pence" for admission, instead of the usual sixpence.

Spellbound, yet determined to give their last ounce of support to the men – farm hands, labourers, carpenters, gardeners – destined to be Shakespearean actors for one night, the audience waited for the curtain to rise and gave a roar of approval to Mr Burrows as he stood, centre stage, ready to introduce the play.

It was a brilliant success. Newspaper headlines, (and not only the local ones) ran;

'A Remarkable Performance in Many Respects.'

'They Did Admirably!'

'Strong performance despite rural accent coming through'

'A Credit'

'Unbelievable that Country Men could achieve so much.'

The press, the audience, critics, writers, strangers, were of one voice in their praise; but not only for the Men's Dramatic Club. There was generous praise for the inhabitants of Sompting who gave so much by way of encouragement and support to all the activities in their village; praise for the mothers of Sompting who "dared" to write and produce their own plays; praise for the folk-singing groups and for the Morris Men; for the village band sometimes turned "orchestra", and praise for the school, from where it all stemmed.

To Mr Burrows, standing on stage that night, beaming, and proud, who gave what the critics said was a '*commendable performance*' as he connected the story of the play where scenes were omitted, must go the last words. At the conclusion of the evening, after giving the '*vote of thanks*' he remarked to the audience on something that was close to his heart; the fact that the stage production of "Julius Caesar" was one aspect of a real '*continuation school*' at Sompting Village.

And then it happened; after success upon success, and with almost the world at its feet, the meteor that was the school reached its zenith, and was about to fall…

VII. *The Failure of Success ~ 1909-1910*

Their romance held no promise of easy times ahead. He was barely twenty years and she was thirty-seven. It began with a play and, like a play, to Harriet Finlay Johnson and George William Weller it seemed, unreal; make-believe, a fantasy, staged only for dreams; but George Weller was a determined young man and a good match for the vivacious headmistress.

He lived with his parents and five sisters (the two youngest, Lily and Elsie, were scholars at Sompting School), in the wheelwright's cottage situated in the village. His father was a carpenter/wheelwright, and George joined the family business as an apprentice, after leaving Broadwater School. Miss Elsie Weller, the youngest sister, proudly explained to the author that her father and brother made the *'whole cart'*, and later expanded the wheelwright living to include a funeral business.

George Weller was tall, dark and handsome, and he was quiet, thoughtful and independent, even as a boy. He took the part of Brutus in the play so seriously that his family was taken by surprise, not knowing he had a penchant for acting. The sound of his voice could be heard *'booming'* throughout the house hour after hour, as he rehearsed his lines in his bedroom. Both critics and press were lavish in their praise of his performance, the press giving him headline status:

> *'The really exacting part of Brutus was played by Mr George W. Weller with an intelligence and sustained force that marked the performer out as THE MOST DISTINCTIVE FIGURE...*

George Weller as Brutus, Feb 1909.

Possibly the spur to do well in the play was more than a '*latent theatrical ambition*', for early on in the rehearsals he had established a special relationship with Harriet, the producer. His determination to give his best to the performance was well known, and perhaps this explained the fact, (to curious observers), that he often stayed behind after other members of the cast had gone home to discuss his part with her; and perhaps his enthusiasm for the play accounted for their ever growing closeness, and was his reason for spending more time at the school; or perhaps it was 'inappropriate', (especially in that day and age of 'face value morals'), for people to think that anything other than 'drama club business' could be on their minds. Whatever the reason, during those winter months, and up until the performance of the play in February 1909, Harriet and George were left to their own devices.

Courting couples at the time, often found privacy in walking: over the Downs, by the seashore or out in the country. Both Harriet and George were familiar with the area, but Harriet in particular would know the quiet, secluded walks, where their secret would be safe. Unknown to anyone, their relationship progressed, and it was not until the night of the performance, the 16th of February, 1909, that the mask slipped, and at least one person perceived the true nature of things. On that evening, for Harriet and for George – and for all the members of the drama club, exhausted after months of hard work on the play, and now consumed by exhilaration and nervous excitement – the moment of truth had arrived; and in the relationship between Harriet Finlay Johnson and George William Weller, the point of no return.

The strain of the past months was too much for Harriet. Only nine days after the performance, and with rumours about herself and George circulating, the school log book reveals that on the 25th of February, the Head Teacher was '*absent, unwell*'. Two weeks later, burdened by anxiety, she returned to her duties feeling ominous storm clouds gathering around her, and a sense of isolation, the isolation of disapproval.

Preceding the Easter holiday, which commenced on April 7th, came news of the most prestigious award the school had ever received. It was the 'Diploma of Honour', gained at the Franco/British Exhibition, held the previous year (1908), in London. The award, the most coveted one in the whole exhibition, was for children's paintings and other work related to nature study.

The school re-opened after the Easter holiday on April 19th with the Annual Prize Distribution Day on the 22nd. Among other presentations, eight scholars received watches for five years perfect attendance. On that same morning, the 22nd April, the Reverend C. Bokenham – after disagreements between himself and Harriet on the teaching of the subject – began a series of lessons on Church History with various classes. The pattern of regular visitors continued, and included visits by Chief Inspector Holmes and other of His Majesties Inspectors. There were the usual absences – chickenpox being especially mentioned in the log book – and Harriet continued to attend meetings of the Advisory Committee in Chichester.

On the 31st April the scholars were given the usual half-day holiday to gather flowers for the May Day celebrations, but there is no mention in the log book of the actual day. Visits by the Vicar, the Reverend Bokenham, appear to be more frequent, and a most disturbing sign that there are problems at Sompting School is an entry in the log book dated May 19th;

> *'Shed containing wood, coal, and old desks, at rear of school burned during the night. No cause discerned'.*

Harriet's handwriting – as she makes entries in the log book – is not as neat as before, and there are several alterations which suggest that her mind was 'elsewhere'; but she did remember to record on June 14th (albeit with an alteration)

> *'The 12th anniversary of my commencement of duties at Sompting School'.*

Absences of scholars, (mainly influenza and ring worm cases), and staff, continued to be a problem;

> *'Miss Godball absent from duties suffering from laryngitis and bronchitis'.*

and a week later;

> *'Miss Godball returned – but as the day was wet and cold I sent her to consult the Doctor. He has now certified her as fit.*

Sports lessons were resumed in the field beside the school, and the girls were introduced to Basketball, *'which they enjoyed'*, while the boys played cricket.

July 1909, and the friction that existed between Harriet and the Vicar over the teaching of Scripture History now erupted into a serious disagreement. Apparently he had his own strong views on how the subject should be taught and, regardless of the head teacher's reservations, put them into practice. It would be small comfort to Harriet, later in the year, to read in the Diocesan Inspector's report that the teaching of 'Bible History' had hardly received its full share of attention.

July 22nd 1909, and Harriet, as if with relief that her struggle to reach the end of term was over, celebrated by a return to her neat, florid handwriting, as she recorded the entry:

July 22nd *School closed for August Holidays*
(Aft.) *(5 weeks)*

But her sense of relief was for more than the end of her most traumatic and heart breaking term; she was relieved that she had finally made a decision about her future; as a result of which, she would soon be seen in public on the arm of the man she had promised to marry, George William Weller.

The occasion of their first public outing together was the wedding of George's sister, in August 1909. The Weller family approved of Harriet, and made what was a difficult time for the couple bearable, by giving them their wholehearted support. Harriet's mother and sister Emily were also invited to the wedding, which turned out to be a happy, memorable day for everyone. Elsie Weller, 12 yrs old at the time, was one of the bridesmaids. She remembers feeling delighted but 'in awe' of the fact that her headmistress (whom she loved), was there as her brothers 'intended' and would soon be her sister-in-law.

Returning to school on August 30th 1909 must have been easier on Harriet than the term immediately preceding the summer holiday. Decisions had been made, and there was now no need for secrecy. During the coming weeks and months however, she had several hurtful encounters and *'spates of jealousy'* to contend with, all intended, no doubt, to unnerve her. She was aware of a comment made in the village: *'I don't know what she wants to get married for at her time of life'*, and how upset George was by a note he received from Bessie, a young neighbour. Bessie 'fancied' him and wrote that she wondered if he knew what he was doing marrying someone old enough to be his mother.

Mary Honeywill, on the scene as usual, and closely involved in school, church and village affairs, had never ceased to be the 'thorn in the flesh', where Harriet was concerned. It was 'enough' when she discovered that Harriet had organised the 'Young Men's Dramatic Club' and was the producer of their play at the Worthing Theatre Royal; but it was the 'limit' when she realised that the rumours and 'innuendoes', rife over past months, were true, and that Harriet and George Weller were indeed 'walking out'. She immediately visited the Weller home, the Wheelwright's cottage on West Street, Sompting. Interrogating Mr and Mrs Weller about the 'affair', she stated bluntly that it must be stopped, and tried to persuade them to '*not approve of the marriage*'. Their simple, quiet answer to her tirade, that they didn't see any reason why George and Harriet should not be married, infuriated her almost beyond reason.

Parents remained closely involved in Sompting 'Continuity School'; and to Harriet's delight and to her credit, many had at last accepted the importance of homework as a necessary 'back up' in the education of their children. There were a few however, who remained to be convinced. One girl complained bitterly that her mother made her – after completing other daily tasks – hem stitch part of a bed sheet, before being allowed time to do her homework.

The progressive work of the school continued with the 'new education': correlated lessons, nature rambles and educational visits, library mornings and, whenever possible, lessons out of doors. Cookery, handicraft, art and a variety of subjects presented in a variety of ways continued to appear on the timetable, and woven throughout, an integral, stimulating source – the drama. With Harriet pre-occupied and worried by external pressures and circumstances, it was as well that the new education was firmly established, the scholars themselves being the custodians. Many years had passed since that first nature ramble, and now the freedom and autonomy that had gradually been bestowed on the children was accepted as a right. So engrossed were they in their school life that they were constantly planning schemes for and around lessons; activities centred on lessons and lessons centred on activities. There were scholars who, distance permitting, met after school to pursue their work, and older ones who felt privileged to be allowed to 'stay in' after school hours, to complete work; scholars joined together in an assortment of activities including 'making up their plays' (usually for lessons) and inventing new ones.

> *'What struck me most forcibly always was the fact that nothing – the amount of preparation, the arrangement of multitudinous details, the memorising of long, long parts, or the making of copious notes – ever seemed to be looked upon as the least trouble. The truth was all these things constituted healthy brain and bodily activity for normal children.'**

The old schoolroom had witnessed amazing scenes in recent years and played its part in unfolding dramas: sheltering weary soldiers as they made their way home from the Crusades; blinds drawn, grasses strewn over the floor, simulating the dank, gloomy castle where Mary Queen of Scots lived out her last days; echoing to the cries of natives and travellers fighting their way through the jungles of Africa; celebratory, as royal processions wove their way through London, the 'crowds' standing on forms for a good view.

---

* Harriet Finlay Johnson – 'The Dramatic Method of Teaching' p.205

'and so real was it to them that they whispered excitedly 'here they come, here they come".

Within five minutes the schoolroom could become a railway station; a Swiss village; a lead mine; a joyous occasion, an office, or the scene of a tragedy. Drama, the medium through which, as Harriet Finlay Johnson had proved, the participants could acquire vast amounts of knowledge, and experiences priceless in their breadth and depth.

But when the plays were over, and the excitement had abated, (and profound lessons absorbed and stored safely in the memory), satisfied, the children were content to be themselves once again in their own familiar surroundings; the school bell sitting as usual on top of the teacher's tall desk; the worn table pressed securely against the back wall of the schoolroom; the blackboard sitting comfortably on its easel; the palm, tall in its brightly coloured pot, standing impassively in the corner near the doorway; the schoolroom having played its part, returned to normal.

The school drama, enacted by enthusiastic, carefree children, would possibly help to alleviate the pressures of the real life drama Harriet was confronted with every day; drama in which she fought to keep her dignity and her authority, in an increasingly delicate and deteriorating situation.

'In building a picture of how it was, every scrap of evidence, every incident, adds lustre to the telling'; and the school log books may offer evidence of more than the actual words read

while scanning the pages. Perhaps the entry for November 4th, 1909, which is a copy of a report received from the Board of Education and has as Item 2

> *'The Board observe that the school registers were only verified by the Managers on one occasion during the last school year.'*

reinforces the suggestion already made that some of the Managers did not like Miss Finlay Johnson. The date on the page is badly smeared suggesting tears had been shed. Not used to adverse reports, might we assume that there were tears shed during the writing of this entry, and tears for those other entries where it is obvious that all is not well at Sompting School.

On November the 4th, 1909 Harriet received a copy of the Diocesan Report, which began with praise for the school then continued with:

> *'But they (the children) are not quite up to the average in general religious knowledge, and the absence of all written work, and of special repetition in the upper division is unusual.'*

Even after this scathing report, we read in the log book: *'The Vicar gave his 'usual scripture lessons'*. The many difficulties Harriet Finlay Johnson had to overcome in her role as headmistress at Sompting School – difficulties which were now compounded by the cruel criticism of her private life – left her feeling drained and humbled; and with a moral so low she despaired of ever looking up again.

In December 1909, Harriet gave notice of her intention to resign from her position as headmistress at the school on March the 4th, 1910. This would give her one month in which to prepare for her wedding, planned for April the 6th. Chief Inspector Holmes was dismayed when he heard of her intention to resign. He did his best to persuade her to change her mind, but to no avail. At the time, it was expected that a woman teacher would leave the profession on marrying, but it was not law that she had to do so. After her marriage, she could remain in her position, 'at the discretion of the local education authority'. During a meeting of the West Sussex Education Committee – after Harriet had given notice of her intention to leave – regret was '*publicly expressed*' that the neighbourhood would suffer a severe loss by the retirement of Miss Harriet Finlay Johnson. She was described as '*a most exceptional teacher*', and the school as being conducted on '*exceptional lines*'. The Education Committee statement continued with:

> '*Miss Johnson's original methods of instruction have proved remarkably successful. They have been designed to stimulate the intelligence of her scholars, and the school has gained a wide fame, quite exceptional in the case of a village school. Learning has proved* A POSITIVE DELIGHT *to the children placed under Miss Johnson's care.*

A reminder was also given, in a statement to the press, of her work being so highly regarded that examples of it were exhibited at the White City; and that specimens of work, accompanied by details of the method of teaching, had even been sent – at the special request of the Board of Education – to be part of a permanent exhibition in Japan. Strong words of praise and approval, but with no suggestion or 'hint' that she might be asked to stay on at Sompting School to continue her '*exceptional*' work. The term ended in sombre mood, with no mention in the log book of plays, or entertainments; of parties, or special church services; of illnesses, or absenteeism, or indeed without mention of any little anecdote often found recorded at the close of previous years. Even the weather failed to be commented on this end of term, Christmas 1909.

January, 1910, and the sombre mood of the Christmas term continued when the school re-opened on the 10th after the holiday. Illness was rife, and by the 21st. of January, twenty one scholars, (and Miss Godball), were absent, '*ill with influenza*'. On the 24th. January the Vicar instructed that the school should be dismissed for one week '*owing to the number absent with illness*'.

In his monthly letter to parishioners, dated January 21st. (published in the Sompting Church Magazine), the Vicar, the Reverend C. Bokenham, wrote of his:

> *'great surprise at the resignation of Miss Harriet Finlay Johnson, and the announcement of her approaching marriage.*

And no doubt', he continued, *'a great surprise to the whole village'*. He is generous in his praise of her work, which, he explains, is known *'far beyond the bounds of Sompting'*.

He states that:

> *'although there may be some who are not entirely in sympathy with her methods, about one thing there can be no difference of opinion, and that is the wonderful way in which she has gained the confidence and affection of the children, both boys and girls, whose school days have been days of happiness, as of course they ought to be, but so very seldom are'.*

Most revealing, is a statement he makes at the end of the letter:

> *'Her successor, (Harriet's), has not yet been appointed but 'The Local Education Authority' have agreed to the request of the Managers that we should have a Master, and have sent us the names of four or five such excellent candidates that the difficulty is to choose between them'.*

Shortly after this letter was published (in February 1910), an appointment was made, the choice falling on a Mr Percy G. Blackmore from Compton, Petersfield. Mr Blackmore was a strict traditionalist.

Gradually, by the end of January, most scholars had returned to school and except for a few ring-worm cases, and the worry of Scarlet Fever, which was in the area, lessons carried on as normal. Children, not able to comprehend the immediacy of Harriet's departure, or the finality that her departure would bring to their present way of life, remained unconcerned and happy. But the main ambition of most scholars would now never be realised. The ambition to be in the *'governess's class'*. Although due to leave the school on March 4th 1910 the authority asked Harriet if she would stay on until the end of term, the 24th. March, by which time her replacement Mr Blackmore would be available to commence duty. She agreed, although it would mean that she had less than two weeks to finalise preparations for her wedding, and the move into her new home, Cokeham Lane House, Sompting.

We see her old flamboyant style of writing in the log book once more as we read:

> *March 21st. 'School 'DIPLOMA of HONOUR' (gained at the Franco-British Exhibition for excellence in school work) framed and hung in school today'.*

and in small script underneath;

> *afternoon; 'Miss Keys absent with a cold.'*

The 24th of March 1910, and Harriet's last day at the school. Once again she recorded in the log book, *'Miss Keys absent'*. But perhaps the absence of the teacher only served to emphasise the singular honour the children bestowed on Harriet.

Every child on the school roll was present, the lessons being conducted in a *'sober atmosphere of reverence and calm'*.

No-one ever discovered the true feelings of Harriet Finlay Johnson on that last day. Outwardly, she was as always, pleasant and smiling, showing a quiet confidence we know – from past months – had often belied an inner turmoil. Maybe we should not try to analyse her feelings, or pry into her thoughts, or delve into the reasons for the 'gloom' we know presided; better to leave the scene to the players, undisturbed; to move quietly away, keeping happier memories fresh in our minds, and remembering the 24th March 1910 not as Harriet's 'last' day at the school, but simply, 'another day'.

She picked up the pen to make her last entry in the log book, marking the end of an important chapter in her life; but as she did so, the page was already turning on to a new chapter, anxious to begin.

VIII. *Epilogue ~ Love Beckons*

> *'When love beckons you, follow him.'* – *Kahil Gibran*

They had a small wedding on Wednesday, 6th, April 1910, with only family and close friends invited, but it was colourful, and it had all the trimmings of a large, splendid affair. The bridal party arrived at St. Mary's Parish Church in a carriage and horses for a ceremony conducted by the Reverend C. Bokenham. Harriet wore a full white wedding gown, with a lace veil covering her head and forming a small train as it swept lightly down beyond the dress; she carried a huge bouquet of spring flowers interlaced with white satin ribbons. The youngest of the three bridesmaids, thirteen-year-old Elsie Weller, wore a cream silk dress and a straw hat trimmed with blue flowers. After the service, the party returned to Harriet and George's new home, Cokeham House, a white, flint stone building in Cokeham Lane, for a sumptuous wedding feast and 'merry making'. The weather in Sompting on that day was recorded as being cloudy and rather cool, with rain at times. Thunder was heard along the coast.

Among the many wedding presents Harriet received was a handsome seven-day mantelpiece clock from Inspector Holmes. The Managers presented her with a purse containing

£11.15.s for which she thanked them, in an open letter addressed to the Vicar:

> *Dear Sir,*
>
> *I desire to convey to the Managers and Subscribers of Sompting School, my very deep gratitude for the gift of a purse containing £11.15.s. It has been very acceptable to me in helping to furnish my new home. It may interest my friends to know that I have placed the money towards buying a Chesterfield Settee and two Grandfather armchairs, which may long serve to remind me of my kind friends on the Management of Sompting School.*
>
> *May I subscribe myself,*
>
> *Yours very gratefully,*
>
> *Harriet Weller.*

The seven-day clock and the Chesterfield Settee were still giving good service in late 1980, in the care of Miss Elsie Weller, at the Wheelwright's Cottage, Sompting, the Weller family home.

Harriet and George quickly settled down into married life. Harriet's mother lived with them at Cokeham House and remained there for the rest of her days. Inspector Holmes persuaded Harriet to write a book about her work at Sompting School. The book, *The Dramatic Method of Teaching*, was published in 1911 by Nisbet & Co, their first venture into educational publishing, again at the instigation of Inspector

Holmes. Published both in this country and in America, and translated for publication in Japan, the book became so successful that Harriet intended to write a second one as a follow up, but this never materialised. She continued her piano practice in a more serious way giving recitals to various organisations and church gatherings, and the new 'Mrs. Weller' (Harriet) was often asked to give talks on education and write for teacher's magazines. In 1918 she was the guest speaker at the 'Oxford New Ideals in Education Conference', but dropped out at the last minute and was replaced by Holmes.

George continued to work in the wheelwright trade, gradually taking over more responsibility for the business from his father; the office was in the Wheelwright's cottage, and after some years, Elsie Weller, his youngest sister, left her secretarial/book-keeping position with another firm to work in the family business. George accompanied Harriet to Hadfield House where they lived for three months when Harriet was employed as private tutor to Lady Betty Hadfield's son. Later, they stayed at Knebworth House for six weeks, where she coached the Earl's son, the third Earl of Balfour. During the six weeks, she staged a play at the House in which she took the part of Queen Elizabeth.

But in all her many and varied activities, at heart she was happiest in the open-air, walking over the Downs with George; (she wrote of the beauty of an evening on the Sussex Downs, either alone, or in the company of a kindred spirit), or on their bicycles touring the countryside. They purchased land opposite their house, which they developed into a chicken farm and an orchard. A few years later, they acquired more land, again nearby, for another orchard and chicken farm, all of which engaged more and more of Harriet's time.

George expanded the wheelwright business to include the designing and making of garden furniture, Harriet using her creative talents to help with the designs. He wrote articles for trade magazines and in 1926, when the wheelwright trade was dying out, he set up in a portable building business, making greenhouses, summer houses, and chicken houses.

Harriet and George got on well together. An uncle of his, and his wife, who had a holiday with them said, "*they live for themselves*". Every year, at family parties, and especially on Christmas Day (tea-time and evening), Harriet was the life and soul of the party; she played the piano, and acted little plays with George's sisters' children, who called her "aunt Dit".

A former scholar at the school when Harriet was headmistress, became her neighbour in Cokeham Lane, for over thirteen years. This 'neighbour' described Harriet as:

> *'always pleasant and smiling; she was helpful and kind, but she remained a very 'private person'; and people in the village were of the opinion that Harriet and George lived only for each other.'*

By 1950 the wheelwright trade had opened out again, and in 1952, George was working in London, preparing a wheelwright's shop, when he became ill. He lay ill in hospital for one month and died there on the 24th March 1952; forty-two years to the day since Harriet's last day at Sompting School. She travelled to the hospital by taxi every day to be with him, accompanied by Elsie Weller, but George wanted no one but Harriet. Harriet herself was recovering from a stroke when George took ill. Fortunately, the stroke did not incapacitate her or affect her mind or her memory in any way. George's sister Annie, who had lived with them for a number of years helping with the housework, stayed on with Harriet after George died.

The following letter, written in April 1955 to two former scholars, Kitty and Winnie, proves that Harriet never forgot her Sompting School days, or lost the love she had for the children:

45, Cokeham Lane, Sompting
8/4/55

My dear Kitty & Winnie,

At last I am writing just a few lines to thank you most sincerely for your pretty card on my Birthday. It was all daffodils and it did bring back to me the happy days at school. I must find a frame to fit it for it really deserves it.

I hope that you are in the best of health, and that God will bless you and keep you.

Look in to see me when you can, and I remain

Your old 'school marm'

Harriet Weller.

Harriet Weller, née Finlay Johnson, 'fell asleep' at her home, Cokeham House, on Wednesday 29th February 1956.

The weather report for that day in Sussex showed it to be a mild but cloudy, breezy day, with possibly light rain in the early evening.

She was buried in St Mary's Parish Churchyard in the same grave as George and his parents, William and Sarah Ann Weller.

Under the long inscription is written one word -- 'united'.

Harriet & George in later life, on holiday.

Harriet's mother, Jane Ann Finlay Johnson.

IX. *Some Other Participants*

To conclude the story of Harriet Finlay Johnson and the little school on the Downs, here is recorded further information on nine of the other participants:

Blackmore, Percy George: Headmaster at Sompting School after Harriet Finlay Johnson. A strict disciplinarian, he was thought of by some former scholars as:

> *'very nice, very straightforward, but a real strict teacher. If you did well you were praised well; if you didn't do well you got the cane.'*

It was said he was unkind to his two daughters, they were always 'in trouble'. Mr Blackmore was forced to leave the school because of a severe caning he gave to one of the scholars.

Herbert, Ethel (nee Riddles): Ethel was the daughter of Edith Riddles (monitress at the school), who first met Harriet in 1937 when she visited the Weller farm to buy chickens. She described Harriet as being very nice but very withdrawn; *'she got to be like a recluse.'* George, as she knew him, was exceptionally quiet. Ethel heard all about the school from her mother, and gathered that Harriet could be strict, but she was a 'GREAT LADY', and that she would be disappointed that her new education came to nothing.

Kennard, Edith (nee Riddles) (1883-1944): Edith Riddles was 14 years old when Harriet arrived at Sompting School, and she was already a popular monitress; (she was the girl with the auburn hair that Revd Bokenham used to hold his hands over saying he was warming them). She was conscientious in her work and caring towards her scholars. Harriet appreciated her efforts and became very fond of her. Entries in the log book give a glimpse of the high esteem in which she was held.

1897

Oct 21st Today Edith Riddles gave a lesson on 'Pens' to Std. III. Notes carefully prepared and lesson given successfully.

Oct. 28th. Edith Riddles, who has assisted in the Mixed department this week, today gave a Lesson on 'The Potato' to Std. III, with experimental allusions to starch as formed from grated potato. Children most attentive and receptive.

1898

March 7th Miss Potter absent with a cold. Her class taken by Edith Riddles (monitress).

Edith stayed on as a monitress probably until the age of 18, when she had a long and serious illness. She eventually married William Kennard in 1912 at the age of 29. William was the eldest in a family of ten, born in Lancing. He left school at 11 years to pick violets in the gardens. Later he joined the

Royal Navy and became an Able Seaman. He courted Edith for 10 years before they finally married, eventually having a son and a daughter, Ethel.

Lindup, Emily (nee Johnson): Harriet's sister and an assistant teacher working mainly in the infant department at Sompting School. She married Harry Lindup, shortly after Harriet's marriage. He was Metellus Cimber and Cassius in the play 'Julius Caesar' performed by the 'Men's Dramatic Club'. His performance was reported by the newspapers as being '*without the least offence to his associates, less pronouncedly rustic than his fellows*'. His brother, Robert Lindup, was Mark Antony in the play. Harry and George were friends, and before they were married, the two of them would sometimes visit London, staying with Harry's aunt; they also did cycle tours. Emily and Harry moved to Surrey after they were married, but Emily often returned to Sompting to visit Harriet and her mother.

Peters, Agnes: Is the tall girl at the back of the photograph captioned, A Nature Study Game. 'Questioning the flowers'. She worked on munitions in the 1914-1918 war, as a result of which she lost her sight.

Shaw, William: The son of Mrs Mary Shaw, a former scholar at the school during Harriet's time. He remembers meeting Harriet when he went to the chicken farm opposite Cokeham House; he was about six years old, (1926). He was with his grandfather who bought baby 'chicks' from the Wellers. Harriet made such a big impression on him that he never forgot either her looks or her manner:

> *'I can always remember – she was a small, sandy-haired person. When I recall her, she was pleasant, happy; only boyish memories but I can remember going up and being taken around and gathering in the small chicks.*
>
> *She would say 'come along, get hold of this, we'll put them in', (packing the little fluffy chicks in boxes) make yourself useful'!*

William always appreciated the fact that Harriet made time to bother with such a young boy and show him how to handle baby chickens.

Stead, Estelle: Shakespearean actress and close friend of Harriet. She toured with Frank Benson's Shakespearean Company and played Shakespearean roles at The Old Victoria Theatre, London from 1914 to 1918. In company with her father W.T. Stead, the writer, she was deeply involved in promoting spiritualism in Britain.

Stead, W.T. (1849-1912) An English journalist who became editor of the *Pall Mall Gazette*, London. He founded the 'Review of Reviews' and worked for peace, spiritualism, the 'Civic Church' and friendship with Russia. He drowned in the Titanic disaster on 15th April 1912.

Weller, Elsie: (1899-1988) Elsie lived well into her nineties. She was the youngest sister of George and a scholar at Sompting School during Harriet's time. Elsie remembered with joy her school days, and continued to be interested in music and drama (interests introduced to her and fostered at school), throughout her long life.

She was a member of a choral society and attended concerts and plays regularly. She lived close to Harriet and George, and became secretary and bookkeeper in the family firm working from home, in 1921. Her own thoughts on Harriet were that she changed after her marriage and that she '*never got over her disappointment that her work had come to nothing.*' Elsie Weller inherited, among other things, the seven-day clock given as a present to Harriet by Inspector Holmes, the Chesterfield Settee, and the two Grandfather armchairs.

Elsie Weller with Harriet's Chesterfield.

2 1872

Decr 13th (Friday) Trying to make a start in arith for below the 1st Class the children appear to have no number in their heads - .

Decr 20th (Friday). Miss Penfold & Mrs Baker took the girls at needle work, 1st time this week. The ordinary lessons given & some improvement observable.

Christmas holiday. a fortnight

1873
Janr 7th The Revd J. B. Honeywill gave a bun to every child in the School, as well as a Cap to each boy & a hood to each girl.

Friday Janr 10th The attendance good, considering the wet weather, & the improvement marked.

Janr 17th (Friday) The elder girls very irregular. Kept at home to assist their mothers, & some of the boys employed in the fields to frighten crows.

Janr 24th (Friday) - Children on the whole very well behaved, but very dull, especially in arithmetic - Fever still in the village, but not spreading among the children -

A page from Sompting School log book, 1872.

1873 3

Jany. 31st One of the elder girls gone to service this week, & several boys engaged in gardens or fields protecting seeds from birds

Feby 7th (Friday) The weather has been wretched the greater part of the week: the roads bad from melting snow, thawing frost & dirt. The attendance low in consequence —

Feby 14th (Friday) Several absent from one or more of the following excuses – "Chilblains", "Colds" "not able to pay school fees" "guarding seeds from birds in market gardens" –

Feby 21st (Friday) Still fever cases among the children – The attendance low in consequence of this, & also because colds & chilblains are very prevalent. The ordinary course of instruction given & satisfactory progress made, considering the above named irregularities

Feby 28th (Friday) A deep snow on Monday & Tuesday – the roads almost impassable from melting snow & slush & mire. A large no of children suffering from colds – fresh fever cases. Altogether the worst school week during the winter.

A page from Sompting School log book, 1873.

410 — 1901

Jan: 14th — Have received letter from Dr. Kempe & have allowed of children (mentioned before) to return to school.

Jan: 15th — Half holiday in consequence of funeral of lad who was scholar in these schools.

" 16 — Half holiday for funeral of Mrs [illegible] a subscriber to the schools & widow of previous Vicar.

" 21 — Dr. Kelly (Med: Officer of health) has directed that the Dukes & Bashfords of Cokeham shall not attend school in consequence of existence of Diphtheria in their neighbourhood.

Jan: 22 — Her Majesty, Queen Victoria (R. I.) died.

25th — Service in the morning at ¼ to 9 o'clock for upper classes, at Church.

28th — All History & Reading Lessons & Obj: lessons until after the

A page from Sompting School log book, 1901.

1902

431

June 23rd The family of Dennetts (See June 9th) have been notified that they may return to school.
During Drawing Lesson this afternoon (being Coronation week) the boys drew "King Edward's Crown" for a drawing exercise.

June 25th No school today, not until July 2nd, in order that teachers and scholars may celebrate the occasion of the Coronation of Their Majesties King Edward VII and Queen Alexandra. The children will have feast and sports on June 26th & will be presented with a souvenir mug.

Cancelled See below

June 25th (Afternoon). School re-assembled, contrary to above entry, in consequence of the sudden serious illness of our beloved King. Feast and sports are abandoned.

" 27th Slight alterations in Register owing to unexpected re-assembly of school.

A page from Sompting School log book, 1902.

1903

449

Nov: 12th The Vicar called and gave me notice of a meeting of Managers (to consider requisitions) on Sat: 14th.

" 19th The children shew much improvement in intelligence since their ~~satisfactory~~ systematic use of their school lenses. St: 3 in particular, (who have been somewhat dull, as a class,) have become fairly proficient in composition, since the introduction of composition on objects.

" 20th The children have made a small collection of money, for the children (scholars) of a poor woman who has died suddenly. I attach importance to this as tending to widen their sympathies. Total sum - 6/6d.

" 25th Policeman called at the school with reference to a case of throwing missiles at a cyclist, which happened on Sat: last. One of the Infants was suspected of doing it.

" 26th Attendance Officer visited. No cases to report.

A page from Sompting School log book, 1903.

1905

469

Sept: 7th — The boys have made a good start in shaded drawing with brush.
Stormy weather slightly upset the attendance this afternoon.

" 15th — Elder classes of boys taken to sketch out of doors this afternoon (model drawing). Start made at 1.30 p.m.

" 21st Thurs: — Miss E.K. Johnson absent with leave this afternoon.

" 22nd Friday — The above again absent some part of the day.
Head Teacher examined lower Standard work (drawing) in connection with Nat: Study. It was specially well done.

" 29th — Simple experiment on Air pressure conducted with Lower Standards. Good results.
A fresh impetus has been given to the oral teaching of Language and expression in Lower school.

Oct: 2nd — Mr Watt (S.A.O) visited. Form 9 received

A page from Sompting School log book, 1905.

1909.

2

Feb: 8th The Revd C. Bokenham (Vicar) visited this afternoon and notified Managers' meeting for Feb: 13th to me. I sent round notices to the several managers.

Feb: 9th Miss Godball sent home from school as she appeared very ill.

" 10th Miss Keys also absent on account of the death of her brother.

" 16th Whole holiday for performance by the village men ~~performance~~ of "Julius Caesar".
Miss Keys still absent. Her mother ill.

" 18th The Vicar visited this afternoon and signed Prize List.

" 25 Head Teacher absent unwell.

March 1st Miss E.R. Johnson took charge of school today.

" 2nd As the Head Teacher is still away the above arrangement continued.

" 4th The Vicar visited.

" 8th Head Teacher returned to her duties. Many children absent ill. One case of chicken pox reported.

A page from Sompting School log book, 1909.